This Journal of
describing our family's long battle with the
Veterans Administration
is dedicated
to our three children,
Sean, Logan and Bryan,
whose very existence
gave me the strength, determination,
and relentless perseverance
to make heart-wrenching decisions
and find the answers needed to protect, feed, educate
and comfort them in circumstances, at times,
unimaginable.
Always know,
Sean, Logan and Bryan,
I thank GOD each day for the
abundant love, joy, and even tears,
we have shared together.
If given the choice....*I would do it all again!*

Our Daily Reminder....

"Making the decision to have a child is momentous. It is to decide forever to have your heart go walking around outside your body."
\- Elizabeth Stone

This Journal of our Family's 19-year battle
with the VA Claims System
is also dedicated to each and every
Veteran and their family
who have experienced similar uphill battles,
while sacrificing their hearts, their souls, and for many,
their lives, for our Country's freedom.

By reading our story, our hope is other Veterans
and their families will come to know peace
they never dreamed possible
- as our family has -
while enduring devastating
and life-changing experiences.

I am also sharing some of our favorite scriptures, quotes
and *"Our Daily Reminders"* from which we continue to gain
immeasurable strength and guidance
so desperately needed.....
*and rarely offered to our Family and so many Veterans and
their Families by the VA.*

While it has been nineteen years since my
Husband's "service-related" death,
with our battle with the VA just as long,
we pray Veterans and their families will come
to learn - as we did -
GOD is offering HIS guidance to each of us....
we simply have to listen.

The lyrics to my favorite song are true,
as GOD truly does....
"Bless the Broken Road!"
To all Veterans and their Families....

Table of Contents

INTRODUCTION…"You Do Not Have a Name."

INTRODUCTION
"YOU DO NOT HAVE A NAME"

I used to pray for somebody to speak out, stand up and voice the concerns of so many Veterans and their families like ours. Then I realized....*I am somebody.*

– derived from quote by Lily Tomlin, Actor

In early 2000, while taking a baccalaureate speech class, we were instructed to prepare a statistical presentation regarding a public agency. I chose the **Veterans Administration**. I began my speech with the following:

"I would like to introduce myself. I am VA File No. XC 28 918 810; U. S. Court of Appeals for Veterans Claims Docket No. 08-4275. Just like thousands of Veterans and their families, I am only a file number to the Veterans Administration's Claims System... I do not have a name."

Instead of relaying numbers and statistics regarding the Veterans Administration – as requested by the Professor - I then took the cover off a family portrait I had brought to class.

i.

I proceeded to tell the class a story - one I would like to share with you now - in honor of all Veterans and their families....*who each have a story of their own.*

My Husband of sixteen years, *James Anthony Caldon*, the Father of our three children, served with the Navy Seabees Mobile Construction Battalion in Vietnam in 1968. He earned National Defense and Vietnam Service Medals.

In January 1987, while we were building our dream home on ten acres of land just outside Chapel Hill, North Carolina, our lives, as we knew it and dreamed of for many years, suddenly disappeared ....*forever.*

ii.

My Husband was diagnosed with Stage IV, non-Hodgkin's lymphoma – later certified by the VA as *"service-related due to exposure to herbicide"* - commonly known as *"Agent Orange."*

Our young children were just 2, 4 and 6 years old.

With my children's blessings and permission, I am sharing with you very personal and life-changing events in our lives that we hope – as a family – will strengthen yours, as they did ours. We learned as a family, you simply have to choose to recognize and acknowledge the *"missions"* and battles GOD has asked you to accept graciously – *even when they are missions and battles you never wanted or asked for.*

My husband had his favorite song *"The Impossible Dream"* sung at our wedding on 31 May 1980. As a result of his "service-related" death from exposure to Agent Orange and the horrific indifference and incompetence of our government's VA Claims System, we came to the realization - the dreams Jim and I had together were, indeed, *"impossible."*

I am now in my nineteenth year fighting the horrific paperwork and total disregard to the facts by the VA Claims System. No matter how long it takes, I will continue to encourage all Veterans and their Families to live each day remembering....through relentless faith, love, and perseverance, your family, just like ours today, will, one day, know, ***"The Impossible Dream"*** is, indeed, **"Possible."**

Our Daily Reminders…

"With GOD, all things are Possible."

– Matthew 19-26

"For we are GOD's workmanship, created in Christ Jesus to do good works, which GOD prepared in advance for us to do."

– Ephesians 2:10

CHAPTER I. A "KNIGHT" TO REMEMBER

Have you ever really listened to the lyrics to the song, *"The Impossible Dream?"*

Among them are…..

> *"This is my quest, to follow that star ...*
> *No matter how hopeless,*
> *no matter how far...*
> *To fight for the right,*
> *without question or pause...*
> *To be willing to march into Hell,*
> *for a Heavenly cause."*

As I mentioned in my Introduction, Jim, my husband of sixteen years, had *"The Impossible Dream"* sung at our wedding on 31 May 1980. Little did we know, his service as a Navy Seabee for our Country would result in his exposure to Agent Orange in Vietnam. Our lives together would, indeed, be *"The Impossible Dream."*

It has now been thirty-six years since Jim and I first met. I received a phone call in 1979 from Jim's older sister - who I knew casually - a call that I did not realize would change my life – and the lives of so many - *forever*.

She called to simply invite me to join a group of her friends who were taking her brother, *Jim,* who was visiting from his engineering work in Saudi Arabia, out for the evening.

Jim's sister had recently gone through a very difficult divorce and he had flown in to simply visit and bring her some comfort – though, according to his sister, his visit would be brief – as he needed to return to his construction work in Saudi Arabia.

Or so we thought.

I will never forget the advice given to me that first night by his sister. She said, emphatically, to me, *"Remember, Denise, don't get interested. He's not staying!"*

While I recall knocking on my friend's door that night, most of all, I remember her brother's smile as he opened the front door. We were both immediately caught off guard. We did not let anyone know that evening about the *"magic"* that had caught us both completely off guard!

A few weeks later, Jim called and asked me to go to a dinner theatre in Atlanta for Easter. I said I would love to. I asked him what his sister and her friends would be wearing.

Jim responded with, *"They are not joining us, Denise. It's just you and me."*

Our first date was Easter, 1979.

Several months passed, and Jim's *"brief"* visit to Georgia was much longer than anyone expected. Being the *"independent"* spirit, I decided to move to Atlanta for a job as I was not yet certain if any future would evolve for Jim and me. And, with my increasing attraction to Jim, I simply did not want to set myself up to be hurt.

My *"going away"* party at the apartment of my twin sister, *Dianne,* was planned! I had casually invited Jim to drop by - not knowing if he even cared to attend. After the party had well begun, I looked around and, unexpectedly and to my total surprise, *in walked Jim.*

I felt like a high school girl on her first date! I tried so hard to act nonchalant and unaffected. Jim appeared to be doing the same.

After several or more glasses of some *"potent"* punch, Jim asked me if I wanted to go *"jogging."* It was 11:00 p.m. at night!

I will never forget that night of *"jogging"* as long as I live. It was truly like a love story novel.

After walking for awhile, Jim suddenly took me in his arms and said, *"Denise, I cannot stop thinking about you!"*

I didn't know if Jim even remembered my name!

That night, I truly thought I had died and gone to heaven. Yes, *we were in love…….*

I did move to Atlanta, but it only proved how much our love for each other had grown. The next few months resulted in many Macon-to-Atlanta trips, champagne, long good-byes, long kisses and passion truly few have known in a lifetime.

In less than three months, following my move to Atlanta, I moved back to Macon so Jim and I could see each other more often. Jim even took me on a *"whirl-wind"* trip to Chapel Hill, North Carolina – to show me his newly acquired land - *where he wanted to build a home one day.*

We then drove to Washington, D.C., his hometown of Agawam, Massachusetts and back to Georgia. Since Jim had lived in Washington for about five years, he knew all the best places to take me in the twenty-four hours we had. We even had dinner at the infamous *"Watergate."*

One thing I learned quickly about Jim is he was an *"eternal optimist!"* A characteristic so rare, and one of the many reasons I fell in love with him.

I learned about this trait while in Massachusetts on our next trip. We were eating dinner, thinking we had plenty of time before our flight left at 8:00 p.m.

Jim decided about 5:00 he had better verify our flight plans – *only to discover our plane was leaving in forty-five minutes!*

It not only takes at least that long to get to the airport, but we still had to stop by *"Sister Ellen's"* Convent to pick some personal keepsakes. Sister Ellen is a Nun Jim knew through his Catholic childhood upbringing who was very special to the Caldon Family.

Upon our discovery of the flight schedule, Jim said, *"Don't worry, just finish your dinner and enjoy."*

After eating, Jim looked at me with that look (I soon learned to know well) and said, *"Since you're through eating – now we'll race to the airport!"*

Jim grabbed my arm. My feet didn't touch the ground all the way to the car! I knew it would be useless to talk him out of this near impossible attempt, so I secured myself in our rented car, and prayed - a lot - as we drove off.

We flew into the Convent, picked up the things we needed, and were off again!

We had about fifteen minutes to board a plane that was scheduled to take off in less than ten! As Jim parked the rented car, I ran into the airport where they said, *"No problem, your flight was detained for 15 minutes."*

When Jim walked up, he was not at all surprised. He simply said, *"I knew we could do it!"* His confidence, passion for life and enthusiasm were traits I grew to love about him more and more.

On July 4, 1979, Jim planned a celebration for Independence Day. We had a picnic, fireworks and even an old-fashioned blueberry pie eating contest at my twin sister's apartment complex for the neighborhood kids. To Dianne's and my surprise, Jim had also planned a *"pre-birthday"* surprise party the same day since our birthday was only a week away.

Jim brought a big, beautifully decorated cake to the picnic table. Only when I tried to cut it, *the cake just bounced up and down!*

With Jim's unique and original sense of humor, *he had a piece of foam rubber cut and fully decorated as a birthday cake at the bakery!* You can see my twin sister's reaction. If you are not sure which one is which, Dianne is the one on the right in the photos above.

To complete our July 4th celebration, Jim got a three-foot cylinder from his car. *He told us it was dynamite!* After much panic and laughter, Jim *"lit it up!"* We were relieved to find out his *"dynamite"* was really a safe, but fun, smoke bomb.

And, yes, Jim later brought out a real birthday cake for all of us and the children to enjoy. Moments like these became very common and almost a daily routine!

As Jim and I grew more and more in love, we also experienced, together, some very sad and tragic times.

On September 5, 1979, as Jim and I sat down to dinner, my Father called. Without any warning, and through much anxiety, grief and tears, my Father managed to spill out the words.... ***my sixteen-year old brother, Craig, had been killed in a car accident.***

I cannot put into words the pain involved in such a sudden, unexpected tragedy. I recall Jim and me jumping in the car and rushing out to the Wednesday night church service where I knew my twin sister would be to tell her the news.

When Jim walked into the church to tell her, Dianne could tell immediately something terrible had happened. She looked Jim in the eyes and said..... *"Anyone but Craig!"*

The next several weeks were like a bad dream - *one I do not care to remember.*

Four days later, Jim and I returned to the house I was renting. The dinner we had sat down to eat together a few days earlier was still on the table....*untouched.*

I grew up a lot during this time. Along with my strong faith in GOD and the strength of my family and friends, I slowly became to realize....*"death is a part of life."*

Little did Jim and I know....***death was already creeping up to our door and would be knocking when we least expected it.***

Jim was 32 years old and very much a bachelor; however, love prevailed. We were falling more in love each day.

In November of 1979 Jim and I talked about getting married. We took his Mother's wedding ring to a jeweler and had it reset. Jim told me I could not see the resetting until he was *"ready"* to be engaged.

I had high hopes we would get engaged at Christmas. However, Jim was not so predictable. After opening all my Christmas gifts, and feeling very disappointed there had been no engagement ring *"under the Christmas tree,"* Jim kept asking me if I *"wanted more coffee."* He was so insistent, I finally said, reluctantly, *"O.K."* And there it was – *in the bottom of the coffee cup* – his Mother's wedding ring – now my reset and gorgeous engagement ring!

14.

We had our dream wedding at *St. Joseph's Catholic Church* in Macon, Georgia on 31 May 1980. Our honeymoon was spent in Chapel Hill, North Carolina where the ten acres of land on the Haw River Jim had bought during his work in Saudi Arabia was located – and where he wanted to build our dream home one day.

And, we did.

Jim called our home – which we built together over the next ten years – ***"Camelot."***

Our Daily Reminder....

"Don't let it be forgot, that once there was a spot –
For one brief shining moment - that was known as
Camelot."

– Alan Jay Lerner, *Camelot: Vocal Selection*

16.

CHAPTER II. LEGACY OF THE HEARTS

Being born and raised an Irish Catholic from Massachusetts, Jim wasted no time taking steps to acquire his lifetime dream of having *"ten children!"* I was forewarned by many members of his family that Jim would keep me *"barefoot and pregnant!"*

We were very excited about having children. On 11 August 1980 – just three months after our wedding – I began writing a Journal.

The first entry says…..***"This journal is dedicated to our children, not yet born, in hope they will know the extraordinary love in which they were conceived."***

Our first born, *a son*, arrived 14 March 1981 – just ten months after our wedding!

Jim had told me that he dreamed of having a son while serving in Vietnam and had his name already chosen. Jim named our son *"Sean-Patrick Anthony"* - with *Anthony* being Jim's middle name.

We were overwhelmed with joy with Sean's arrival and already talking about our next nine! In fact, Jim's sister even had children figurines placed on a wooden frame so we could have their names engraved on the plaques as they were born.

Jim and I, *and now Sean*, would spend every weekend and most nights after work traveling from our apartment in Carrboro, North Carolina to our country land in Chapel Hill. We spent our time together cutting trees, picking up branches and clearing most of our ten acres as we prepared to build our dream home.

While I initially had to get used to the idea of having such a large family, Jim's relentless enthusiasm was contagious – quite literally! As soon as I was able to fit back into a pair of jeans after Sean was born, we learned we were expecting again. *We were thrilled!*

In 1981, when Sean was just four months old, a remarkable – and what proved later to be a true blessing during a very difficult period - became a reality.

When Sean was in his baby walker, he kept throwing his toys on the floor. Hearing my frustration, Jim went to the closet, got a curtain rod, attached it to the baby walker and tied toys onto the rod. I took one look and said, *"I know other Mothers can use this!"*

A few days later, I picked up the telephone and called GRACO Children's Products in Pennsylvania.

After much negotiating and taking steps to ensure our rights would be protected without an attorney - as we had no money to pay them – *Jim and I had a signed royalty agreement eighteen months later with GRACO Children's Products for seventeen years!*

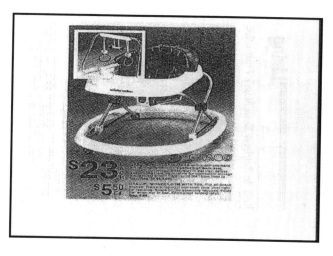

The local newspaper in Georgia even released an article about our toy idea being sold worldwide. We began receiving royalty checks from GRACO Children's Products each quarter – just enough to keep us going - as my husband's dream of building our *"Camelot"* home was one he both lived for each day.

Before Sean's birth, I worked at the *Frank Porter Graham Child Development Center* at the University of North Carolina - Chapel Hill. I worked with a dear and, now, lifelong friend – who I found again recently on Facebook. *Her name is Cathy.*

At the end of my maternity leave, I realized I could not return to work as I wanted to be home with Sean, who was only a month old. However, a second income – before royalty checks began – was critical.

I placed an ad for *"home babysitting."* A person named *"Molly"* answered my ad. With her young son, *Andrew,* my stay-at-home enterprise began. I later added another young boy to our group and learned quickly how to *"multi-task!"*

Molly and my apartment neighbor, *Gay,* also became my life-long friends. They have both *"rescued"* me on many unfortunate occasions and under very volatile and unexpected circumstances which occurred years later. I realize now, *both their friendships were truly GOD sent.*

In November 1982, GOD blessed us with the birth of our second child, a daughter, *Logan Elizabeth.* I will always remember Jim's happiness with having a daughter – so happy he packed our car in Chapel Hill just two weeks after she was born and informed me *"We are going to Georgia to surprise our family!"*

Just like many of our *"whirlwind adventures,"* it was one
I remember with a smile. Jim's sister, *Tina,* who had
introduced us, and my twin sister, *Dianne,* were at a
church dance and did not know we were coming to town.
Jim loved surprises and we simply walked into the
church event with Logan in his arms. That evening
proved to be another *"Knight to Remember."*

After the dance, we arrived at Dianne's apartment where she
called my parents and said, *"Can you come over to my
apartment?"* They did not know she and Jim wanted to
surprise them with our visit as well.

A short time later, my Father and Mother arrived. When my Father saw us, he was thrilled, but quickly went to the other room.

He later told us when Dianne called and did not say why she asked them to come over, my Father had grabbed his loaded firearm so he could confront whoever was disturbing his daughter! With her being a single Mom, my Dad assumed she needed him to deal with an intruder.

Needless to say, we enjoyed the rest of the evening without incident.

A few months later, per Jim's insistence, we purchased a double-wide, modular home and placed it on the ten acres of land "temporarily" to enable us to continue clearing the land on our own as we began building our dream home.

In the spring of 1984, I remember walking up to Jim as he was entering the outdoor shed where he kept his tools and lawn equipment. *I informed him we were, again, expecting!*

He was overjoyed - as his dream of ten children was becoming a reality. And, for him, *the sooner the better!*

Our third child, *Bryan Alexander*, was born in January 1985. I will always remember the joy on Jim's face when he first saw his youngest son – it was as if Bryan was our first. *Jim and I loved our children as much as life itself!*

I had earned my real estate brokerage license and was selling real estate part-time during the children's school hours. Our children attended St. Thomas More – a wonderful parochial school in Chapel Hill.

We were building our dream home and raising three of our ten children.

Life was wonderful!

Our Daily Reminders….

"Children are Gifts from the Lord."
                                        - Psalm 127:3

"Blessed indeed is the man who hears many gentle voices call him 'Daddy"
                                        - Lydia Maria Child

CHAPTER III. "THE IMPOSSIBLE DREAM"

Little did we know, just two years later on *27 January 1987,* the course of our lives would change dramatically. The emotional, physical and financial toll to our *"All-American"* family would be overwhelming.

Just one year after we were married, I noticed Jim doubling over in pain after eating something as simple as a slice of apple. I recall one event in which he had to pull the car to the side of the road as he was having excruciating pain in his abdomen.

I wrote in my Journal on 6 July, 1981:

"This past week Jim was in the hospital because of some internal bleeding. The cause was never found, but he is doing much better."

Over the next few years, these episodes began happening frequently. We decided it was time for him to have a medical evaluation. I recall the initial doctor telling me privately that my husband's symptoms were *"psychological."* I was hesitant to question the doctor's medical diagnosis, but I knew Jim was in real physical pain.

After a few more months, the pain increased, and we sought a second opinion at the University of North Carolina Memorial Hospital in Chapel Hill. Jim's initial tests did not determine any cause.

In early January of 1987, as we were still living in the modular home in the country and building our dream home, Jim's stomach pains persisted. His doctors advised him to undergo exploratory surgery to determine if he has a possible hernia or appendicitis.

Following Jim's surgery, I returned to our home in the country to check on my Mother who had driven to Chapel Hill from Macon, Georgia to help look after our three young children so I could stay with Jim during his medical procedure and recovery.

I remember that day in January 1987 as if it was yesterday…..

Excerpt from my Handwritten Journal dated 1987:

"The morning of January 27, 1987 will be with me for a long time. I had planned to go to the hospital around 10:00 a.m. but I called Jim to see how he was doing around 8:00 a.m. He really didn't seem himself. He sounded confused, somehow different. After hanging up, I just couldn't let go of the feeling that something was wrong…..very wrong."

"I called back to the hospital and had his surgeon paged. I explained my feelings and asked if he had any possible explanations. In a very neutral and "matter-of-fact" voice he said that he had visited Jim earlier, but that he was asleep. And, yes, by the way, pathology indicates that Jim has lymphoma."

"No forewarning, just a statement. My world crashes down with a word - one word ....lymphoma."

I was speechless and numb.....

I quickly composed myself and begged the oncologist to *"Please wait to tell Jim when I am with him. I am leaving now for the hospital."*

His response was, *"We are a research hospital. We have to teach medical students how to inform patients they are terminally ill. Your Husband has Stage IV, non-Hodgkin's Lymphoma. He has two years to live. We are going down the hall now to tell him."*

I pleaded, once again, for the surgeon to wait for me before he told Jim the prognosis. He agreed, but only if I came immediately.

My adrenalin kicked in. I left the children with my Mother with no explanation. I jumped into my car and raced back to the hospital.

I remember it was snowing outside and the roads were barely drivable.

As I drove, my mind kept saying, *"This cannot be happening! Jim is only forty years old! We have three young children! We are planning to have seven more! We are in the middle of building our dream home! How will I tell our children their Father is dying!?"*

I remember walking down the hospital corridor alone. I was suddenly in a whole new world - *one of grief and shock.* I wanted to wake up from the nightmare, but reality was setting in. I composed myself, and walked into my Husband's hospital room. I found myself surrounded by over twenty medical students - *who were there to learn how to tell a patient they are dying.....*

The surgeon had at least waited for me to arrive so I could be with my Husband when they gave him the news.

Jim accepted the news from the surgeon with much grace. As I look back, I realize...he, too, was in shock. Our whole life and the lives of our children changed forever - *with only a moment's notice - and with no warning.*

As soon as the surgeon and medical students left the room, I had time to speak with my Husband privately.

I then went out into the hall and found a phone (this is before cell phones) to contact *Dr. James F. Smith, Jr., Oncologist, M.D., F.A.C.P* – also, my brother. Jimmy lived in my hometown of Macon, Georgia. Our conversation resulted in Jimmy consulting with the Chapel Hill Oncologists on various areas of a very complex – and in Jim's case – *a very advanced disease and terminal illness.*

Once Jim was released from the hospital, the regiment of routine chemotherapy treatments - *most experimental -* began.

Before the ultimate loss of his hair, Jim wanted very much to have a professional family photo taken of us on the UNC-Chapel Hill campus grounds. This very special photo represents the *"beginning of the end"* of the dreams Jim and I had together for so many years – dreams we believed would last a lifetime.

GOD simply had other plans.

OUR DAILY REMINDER....

"For I know the plans I have for you," declares the LORD, "plans to prosper you and not to harm you, plans to give you hope and a future."

- Jeremiah 29:11

During this grueling reality and transition, one of our neighbors was not happy our modular home was still on the property as it was past the date mentioned in our verbal agreement to have the unit moved from the property. The date to move our modular home was no longer possible due to Jim's unexpected terminal illness and subsequent treatments and, at times, overnight stays at the hospital.

When we explained to our neighbor Jim had become ill, she said it was a *"lie"* and we *"were just making his illness up."* She reminded us we had *"passed the deadline for having the modular home moved from the property."*

Our neighbor later filed a lawsuit, which we had to address during my Husband's extensive chemotherapy treatments. I thought my Husband's drastic weight loss and loss of hair would confirm his terminal illness was, indeed, *real.*

She simply did not care.

Jim's brother, *Eddie*, and his wife, *Nancy*, had sent Jim a large piece of tractor equipment to help Jim work on the construction of our new home during his chemo treatments as we, together, did much of the initial work ourselves. *"Sweat equity"* was what it was called and we had plenty of that!

We would clear the land from morning to dark, while the children played in the tree house Jim had built. We traditionally had annual *Fourth of July* celebrations on our land as well. Jim would borrow a large flag from Chapel Hill's Engineering Department and spend hours raising it between trees. We loved teaching our children about the military service their Father had given – and trying to explain to them, **he would be paying the ultimate sacrifice one day.**

I remember one 4ᵗʰ of July, Jim's brother and sister-in-law came all the way from Massachusetts to celebrate with us – and slept in the tree house overnight. Jim and I even served them *"breakfast in bed"* the next morning!

During these very difficult financial times, I came to the realization the toy idea to which Jim and I sold the rights to GRACO Children's Products in 1982, was GOD's way of helping our family financially in the years ahead during Jim's terminal illness.

One day I noticed we only had ten dollars in our checking account. Yet, we had new home construction underway and bills far beyond my salary as a part-time real estate Broker and my husband's partial VA disability benefits.

I felt I had no other alternative but to pray.

And pray I did.

I literally sat down and talked with GOD and told him I had simply done all I could do. Our bills were now *"in HIS hands."*

That day, I literally *"let go,"* and handed my *"troubles"* completely over to GOD.

The next day I called the accountant at GRACO Children's Products and asked them why our quarterly check was late. We were desperate and literally had no money for food for our three young children.

To my complete surprise, the GRACO Accountant said they discovered recently we had *"not been paid for years of royalties from the sale of our toy being sold overseas"* and they were *"re-calculating our quarterly royalty check."*

Our quarterly GRACO check arrived a few days later.

The check was for $89,000!

The government, of course, received a large portion in taxes; however, if I had sat down and added up all our construction, household, school tuition, child-care bills, and more, it would have been about $49,000 – which is exactly the amount we ended up with.

From that moment on, I have never doubted GOD does, indeed, listen. We simply have to trust HE will answer our prayers – in HIS time.....*not always ours.*

As a result of Jim's terminal illness diagnosis a few years earlier, his very aggressive chemotherapies – including the Interferon shots I was now required to give him at home – were extensive. They were taking a major and lasting effect on my Husband's physical, mental and emotional stability.

That said, it is important to note, the details I share now describing events our three young children and I experienced during my Husband's terminal illness were the direct result of Jim's Stage IV, non-Hodgkin's lymphoma disease, PTSD (Post-Traumatic Stress Disorder), and experimental chemotherapies ....*not him.*

Jim was a loving and dedicated Husband and Father – who, *through no fault of his own*, was forced to slowly die before our eyes as a result of his horrific and devastating exposure to a lethal herbicide during his brave service for our Country.

We later learned from the Medical Assessment from *Oncologist, Dr. James Smith*, as a result of clinical trials, some of the chemo drugs Jim were given – including the Interferon shots given at home – are believed to cause *"severe depression, psychological decline and psychiatric decompensation."*

These drugs contributed significantly to our family **"losing"** my Husband, my children's Father, emotionally, mentally, and eventually, physically, before his *"final"* death in July 1996 - following a failed bone marrow transplant.

Medical Assessments detailing these facts were submitted to the VA Claims System through the *Board of Veterans Appeals* and the *U. S. Court of Appeals for Veterans Claims* countless times over the last decade. Excerpts from those medical assessments are included in this book.

While we were still living in the modular home during this time, and completing our new home construction, Jim began to detach himself from me and the children.

For a period of three months, Jim did not utter one word to me, even with our three young children with us each day and our sleeping in the same room every night.

For the emotional well-being of our children, I took each day…*one day at a time.*

The silence was deafening.

I became so concerned for my Husband's mental health, I began researching - when I could find the time. I discovered the following from Goodwyn (1990), entitled, **"Biological Effects of Vietnam Services."**

It says, in part:

"The rage and frustration felt by the Veteran may precede a history of spousal abuse and explosive violence at home. Others, not so severely affected, may continue to live in isolation as partners living under the same roof, yet detached."

After months of prayer and soul searching for answers, I sat Jim down after the children had gone to bed for the night. I said, in essence, *"I love you enough to let you go."*

45.

I told him my twin sister, *Dianne*, would be flying in to help me pack a truck and drive back to Georgia with the children so he could have more time to himself – time to absorb the realities we were all facing, without worrying about us, as he needed to save his energies for himself.

The reality of Jim's mortality arriving at our doorstep far too soon was simply a reality that would bring anyone to their knees in grief.

Jim was simply dealing with this reality through his silence.

After Dianne arrived, and following our finishing packing up the kitchen, Jim suddenly, said to me…. **"Can we talk?"**

We did. He begged me to stay. During this time, I found the yellow note below. It says….

"I hope you know the depth that your love invades my being. I love you. J"

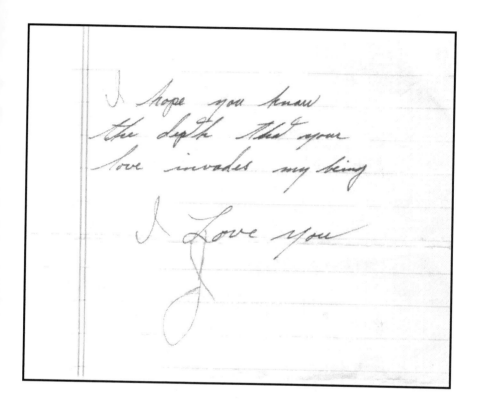

The children and I did not move back to Georgia –
at least, not then.

We were advised by one of the attending oncologists at N.C. Memorial Hospital to schedule meetings with a Psychiatrist. After several meetings together in Chapel Hill, the psychiatrist took me aside and told me privately that Jim was *"stuck"* in several of the stages expected in terminally ill patients - **anger and denial.**

He went on to say, in some cases, terminally patients remain there until the end and **"detach themselves from their family in order to prepare their loved ones for their lives without them in the future."** Jim would, in his opinion, never progress to the *"acceptance"* stage because of the fact he would not be able to see his children grow into adulthood.

Jim rarely spoke about the realities of his Stage IV, non-Hodgkin's lymphoma. While there were months of laughter and joy in our home, his emotional health, mental stability and physical abilities were declining and becoming unpredictable with each day.

According to the American Psychological Association (APA), *"an individual diagnosed with a life-threatening illness, such as cancer, is included in the list of traumatic events"* that can result in **Post-Traumatic Stress Disorder**, commonly referred to as ***"PTSD."***

In addition, The Veterans Health Council describes PTSD as an anxiety disorder that surfaces after experiencing a very dangerous, frightening, and uncontrollable event such as military combat exposure.

Jim had experienced both a life-threatening illness and an uncontrollable event in his military service in Vietnam.

I recall one day when Jim was laying on the couch in our new home covered with a blanket. When I asked him if he was o.k., he responded quietly and slowly said he was remembering *"seeing my best friend blown up in front of my eyes"* in the jungles of Vietnam.

Jim never spoke of that horrific incident again.

The Veterans Health Council further reports PTSD symptoms fall into four categories – most of which Jim displayed increasingly in our daily family life: 1) **avoidance** (amnesia, **dissociation, numbing, hyper-vigilance, controlling behavior, and isolation;** 2) **reliving or re-experiencing (flashbacks,** sleep disorders, overwhelming feelings, and **overreacting**); 3) **victimization (distrust of others, abandonment,** helplessness, and **fear of change**); and 4) shame (feeling guilty, feeling as if you're mentally ill, and feeling unworthy).

I remember looking into Jim's eyes on many occasions and seeing nothing more than a blank stare. Sadly, this had become a daily feature. Several of our friends expressed their concerns to me in private as they, too, had noticed this trait.

One day I was in the tub and he suddenly walked in with a rage of anger and said, *"I am going to kill you!"* He plugged in the hair dryer and threatened he was going to drop it in the tub of water. Then he laughed, and walked out. Jim did not even recall his threatening actions the night before when I brought them up the next day.

The reality of his terminal illness, PTSD symptoms and his experimental chemotherapy drugs were slowly destroying him.....*and my Husband did not even realize it.*

During Jim's frequent treatments, we continued to build our dream home which Jim had designed in its entirety. He had drawn the initial plans on a simple napkin one night as we had dinner out.

It was a masterpiece!

Our "Camelot" home had heated floors, a two-sectional Dutch front door, and a magnificent nineteen-foot stone fireplace with stone from Tennessee. Jim even brought in stone boulders with the tractor his brother had sent to him as a gift to help our family in the construction of our dream home following his cancer diagnosis.

Jim, I, our three young children, the builders that came later, and Curt, our neighbor, signed our names with a sharp edged instrument onto a large green slab of marble – the same as the marble hearth.

Jim had it inserted into the side of the stone fireplace chimney as he wanted this signed piece of marble to be a permanent reminder of the foundation and legacy of a home he had hoped our family would live in for generations.

Jim, still full of surprises, came home one day to tell me he had *"bought a building!"* He had plans to take it down from it's location in Chapel Hill, and transport it to our land for a "barn" as he had always wanted one on our land. It, too, resulted being a *"work of art,"* only it needed painting badly.

Jim did not have the energy, and we did not have the money for a painter, so I spent one full summer on the ladder painting the new *"addition"* to our home baby blue – to match our newly constructed home – both *"labors of love"* - and lots of it!

A very memorable event occurred during this time when Jim was in the middle of his aggressive chemotherapy treatments. Jim was recovering overnight from his recent treatment in the hospital. I received a phone call from a truck driver who said, *"Are you Mrs. Caldon?"* I said, *"Yes. How can I help you?"* He replied, *"I have your four ponies and will be delivering them to you within the hour."*

I thought he was joking!

I immediately called Jim's brother in Massachusetts. I knew, if anyone knew what was happening, it would be him.

Jim's brother informed me "yes" he had sent the children a special gift – *four Irish ponies – Connemaras*!

It was their Uncle and Aunt's way of easing some of the children's anxiety about their Father's illness as they felt the ponies would allow the children to refocus more on the new members of our family. And, for a while, their special ponies did just that......

My brother-in-law and sister-in-law were planning to visit in a few weeks, so I felt, perhaps I could keep the ponies hidden until they arrived. I knew once the children saw the ponies, my time and energies would be redirected for certain.

We did not, yet, have running water at the barn across the street from our home, so every afternoon, for the next few weeks, I carried buckets of water across to the barn to give water to our ponies. When the children asked where I was going, I replied, *"I am putting water in the tractor."*

One day, our daughter, *Logan,* came running up to me while playing outside near her treehouse and said, *"Mom, there are the biggest dogs running around our barn!"*

The "gig" was up!

I introduced our children that day to *Shamrock, Clancy, Cricket* and *Limerick* – who became very treasured *"members of our family"*

Other members of our family were *Bandit* – the baby raccoon Jim had brought home after being rescued from a dog attack in Chapel Hill. Our children enjoyed bringing him back to health and watching him sleep nights in the wreath of our front door. Jim released him a few months later in the woods on our land. *Murphy*, our Golden Retriever, was with our family for many years, along with a countless number of rabbits and hamsters.

I will never forget when we first moved into our new home. The children were suddenly laughing out loud and running around. It did not take me long to find out why.

Jim was giving *Shamrock*, one of our new ponies, a personal tour throughout our new home! He said it was a tradition handed down by his family in Massachusetts.

Logan took dressage lessons for years and won many ribbons and awards. Her love for horses was GOD's way of redirecting our family's energies and focus – and away from their Father's pending death – *at least for a time*.

Our children had two best friends, *Ricky* and *Spencer*, who were instrumental in providing our children with wonderful memories which they cherish still today.

The five of them would play endless hours on the ten acres of land and riding the ponies.

One afternoon, Spencer and Logan had taken off on one of the trails to the Haw River. A short time later, the two ponies returned – *but no Logan and Spencer!*

I was, of course, frantic. I quickly learned the ponies had simply taken off on a hill on the trail too quickly and Logan and Spencer had slipped off. They were fine.

This was a normal afternoon!

Ricky and Spencer were very special, indeed, and GOD's *"gifts"* to our children at a very difficult time in our family's life.

Spencer, Ricky, Sean, Logan and Bryan

Spencer, Bryan, Sean and Ricky

Among our children's fondest memories are the water fights they had with their Dad. There were many, just not enough....as his disease was taking him away.....*literally.*

Yes, there were good times.

They simply did not last long enough...

We were further advised to obtain a child psychologist to assist in preparing our three young children for their Father's terminal illness. We were introduced and hired *Dr. Carolyn Schroeder, ABPP Clinical Child and Adolescent Psychologist* in Chapel Hill. Our family went to her office and she visited our home in the country often.

Dr. Carolyn Schroeder stated in her Medical Assessment submitted to the VA Atlanta Regional Office, the Board of Veterans Appeals (BVA) and the U. S. Court of Appeals for Veterans Claims, in part:

"Over the course of his disease and treatment he changed from a loving, caring and compassionate person to one who was clinically depressed and exhibited erratic and unpredictable behavior including verbal and physical abuse of his wife. The children were often witness to this behavior and, at times, he put them in potentially dangerous situations."

One night, the children and I were alone in our new home out in the country. It was soon after dinner time, and I had not seen Jim. The phone rang. It was Dr. Schroeder.

Dr. Schroeder said to me, *"Whatever you are doing, leave your home now and take the children with you - NOW!"*

I asked her *"Why?"* Dr. Schroeder said she was not at liberty to explain, but told me again to *"Get the children and leave the house immediately."*

I remember driving quickly from our country home to my friend Molly's home in Chapel Hill. She always opened her heart and her home to the children and me during times like the one that night. I knew she would always be there for me and the children.

As we drove to her home, a statement Jim had said to me a few months earlier came to mind. He said, *"I learned how to dispose of bodies without a trace in Vietnam. They will never find you."*

This was not my Husband talking….this was his disease, the PTSD and the experimental treatments for his terminal illness.

Molly recently wrote a support letter – per the request of the attorneys who now represent me, *Bergmann and Moore* from Bethesda, Maryland - who submitted Molly's support letter to the *Board of Veterans Appeals*. In her letter, Molly detailed many of the events described in my book and support letters from others.

64.

■ Excerpt from friend Molly's Support Letter sent to the BVA and dated 17 September 2014:

"His (Jim) behavior became increasingly erratic and frightening. From then on, Denise shared with me her fear of Jim, with great concern for the safety of her children and herself, to the point that I became very afraid for them as well.

■ Excerpt from Dianne's Support Letter submitted to the VA 24 Oct 2004:

"Toward the end of his battle and in his last survival mode, Jim Caldon chose to leave the family unit for several reasons: One being his anger at being terminally ill and not seeing his children grow up.

Many of his family members believe he chose to detach himself because he loved his family so much he wanted to force them in their new direction and their new life so they could be strong without him."

"Jim Caldon died many years before his death. I saw it. I witnessed it. And I grieve today because of what it did to my sister...for she loved him so much."

■ Excerpt from friend Gay's Support Letter submitted to the BVA in early 2000:

"When Jim was diagnosed with non-Hodgkin's lymphoma in January 1987 (their children were only 2, 4 & 6), his whole world came crashing down. Overtime, he became a stranger to many."

"While I knew in my heart that he always loved Denise and the children, the years and years of chemotherapies and the fact that he would not see his children grow up simply took an awful toll on him...... Please be assured that if there has ever been "An All American Family," then the Caldons were it."

■ Excerpt from Curt's Support Letter submitted to the VA 24 October 2004:

"The union of Jim, Denise and their children was so close knit that I can only conclude that abrupt cessation was the consequences of the emotional strain of year after year of coping with the effects and the therapies associated with terminal illness.......Any decision he took in this disease's later stages could not have reflected his characteristic judgment and devotion to his family."

It was during these very volatile times for our family when I first learned of a woman from Oregon who my Husband had known in high school and dated for a time. She had been married three times and had no children.

My book is not about a woman scorned. The fact my Husband was dying and had a wife and three young children who loved him very much did not stop this person from destroying what little time our family had left to hold onto.

It is about a Veteran's Widow trying to survive while raising three young children alone following the death of her Husband, while the VA moves her file from one desk to another in hopes she will give up.

When I brought the woman from Oregon to the attention of Jim's Psychiatrist, he told me *"research shows terminally ill patients often revert back to old acquaintances they knew in earlier and happier times as the current time is far too painful."* In many ways, they are trying to erase the present as they realize there is no future.

This individual from Oregon was clearly taking advantage of my Husband's very vulnerable state of mind during the short time he had left here on earth – ***time the children and I would have cherished.***

I began coming across *"sexually suggestive"* letters this woman would mail to my Husband to our home in the country - the home in which Jim, me and our three young children lived.

On 18 November 1992, I found a Thanksgiving card this woman from Oregon mailed to my Husband and delivered to our home. It said, *"Are you a legman? A thighman" A breastman?" Or do you just wanna neck? Happy Thanksgiving!"*

I, of course, asked my Husband about this woman; however, at this point in my Husband's illness, my energies and focus had to be primarily directed to our three young children. We had already begun to *"lose"* him even before his ultimate death a few years later.

We separated for a time, but got back together. During this time, the children and I had traveled to Georgia and returned home through Athens, Georgia. While there, we visited the Pottery Barn Outlet store.

When we first walked in, a large Knight caught my eye immediately. I thought, what a wonderful Christmas gift for their Father, realizing, this may be my Husband's last Christmas.

Now, take a minute and try and visualize my hauling this seven-foot sharp metal statue to my family station wagon - with three young children walking beside me through the parking lot. I, somehow, managed to maneuver the Knight through the back end door of the station wagon. Then, I pushed the Knight forward and slid him through the driver's and passenger's front seats. Once he was securely in place, I proceeded to slide our three young children under the Knight's sharp sword and sat them all beside and in back of this very intimidating *"Knight in Shining Armor"* – a gift for their Dad!

Needless to say, we had a very *"uneventful"* trip home - which took about four more hours – as our children were too scared to say a word and too fearful to move an inch!! The fact that the police did not stop me for carrying a lethal *"weapon"* was a miracle!

The Knight was the last Christmas gift I ever gave my Husband.

Our oldest son, *Sean,* now has the Knight in his apartment.

Jim's chemo treatments and frequent doctor's visits had become the norm. I was encouraged by Dr. Schroeder and the Oncologists to have open conversations with our young children, and to have them attend and sit with their Father during his chemotherapies at the hospital... *when possible.*

I picked the children up early from school frequently. I will never forget walking from the hospital parking garage with our three young children and across the closed bridge to the hospital for them to visit their Dad during his treatments.

The trips to the hospital were so often, I could walk the path over the hospital bridge blindfolded.

Letters and cards from the woman from Oregon began showing up again at our home and my Husband's detachment and erratic behavior returned.

His erratic behavior was never truly gone as Jim was having a very difficult time with the realization he was dying…..

The woman from Oregon simply took full advantage of my Husband's weaknesses – as she has done for the past nineteen years with the VA Claims System - allowed by the *Board of Veterans Appeals* and the *U. S. Court of Appeals for Veterans Claims.*

One event is one I have tried hard to forget.

The children and I had just returned to Chapel Hill from a visit to Georgia to visit family and we were suddenly confronted by Jim – who was in a rage and in his car. He demanded that the children be moved from my car to his.

They were very scared. I had never kept the children from seeing their Father, but was increasingly concerned about his unusual behavior in front of them.

This day was no exception.

I immediately locked the doors to our station wagon, and drove from the country to the Chapel Hill Police Station – *with Jim racing behind us the entire way.* It was about a thirty minute drive. Once I got to the Police Station, the Officers on duty calmed Jim down. I later asked for a Police Report and was told the Officers had chosen not to write one up.

During this time, our family became very close to *Dan and Kim,* two of the oncology nurses at the N.C. Memorial Hospital who helped Jim during his initial hospital stay and subsequent chemotherapies.

The children and I have kept in touch with Dan and Kim ever since my Husband's death in 1996. They even attended our daughter's wedding in Tennessee in 2005. Dan and Kim wrote two support letters to the VA about the realities that were unfolding to which they witnessed, firsthand - both at the hospital and at our home in the country.

▪ Excerpts from Dan and Kim's Support Letter sent to the VA 25 October 2004:

"We first met Jim and Denise when Jim was receiving treatment for non-Hodgkin's Lymphoma at UNC Hospital. We were initially just two of the oncology nurses caring for Jim during his stay in the hospital. As we got to know the Caldon family, we were impressed by the relationship between Jim and Denise, and became friends with them outside of the healthcare setting. We watched as Denise dealt with the ups and downs of her husband's terminal illness while still trying to keep a sense of normalcy for their children."........

"We believe that Jim changed significantly from the person we met when he first started treatment at the hospital. Jim didn't display what we considered "normal" coping mechanisms. He withdrew, became almost non-communicative at times and wouldn't even look you in the eye when he did choose to speak."

"He seemed to have this penetrating stare and would look over your head when he spoke. We watched as Jim continued to exhibit behavior that finally pushed his family away at a time when his entire family could have benefitted from the time they had left to spend together."

▪ **Excerpt from Dan and Kim's Support letter sent to the VA 30 August 2007:**

"As is usual when an individual learns he has a potentially life threatening illness, this individual tends to go through a grief process as he or she come to terms with the potential inevitability of their own death.

But Jim was different. Instead of this bringing him and his family closer together, Jim began withdrawing into himself and began pushing his family away. He seemed to become more volatile and less communicative."

Dan and Kim were among the medical personnel, family and friends who submitted Medical Assessments and support letters to the VA Claims System – which were later sent to the BVA and the U.S. Court of Appeals for Veterans Claims. These letters describe in detail the realities that were about to unfold – to which the VA Claims System – beginning with the Atlanta VA Regional Office – has refused to address appropriately for now nineteen years.

I recall a time when Jim went off on another outrage, during which I discovered our oldest son, *Sean*, who was ten years old at the time, had jumped out of his bedroom window and run into the woods.

As a result of my husband's increasing erratic and unpredictable behavior – again, believed to be brought on largely by experimental chemotherapies and PTSD terminal illness and combat experience symptoms, *I was advised by Dr. Schroeder to relocate our young children to a safer environment.*

The very difficult decision to move the children to Georgia was made in August 1993. His exposure to Agent Orange had finally taken my Husband, their Father. In many ways, *he was already gone……..*

I had to also leave my job at the Chancellor's Office at The University of North Carolina in Chapel Hill which I enjoyed very much. I had left my real estate position and taken the job at the University after Jim's medical diagnosis to help with the financial obligations as we were still building our new home and our living expenses – which included our children's school tuition and medical expenses not covered by the VA - were getting out of our control.

78.

OUR DAILY REMINDER ....

"Love bears all things, believes all things, hopes all things, endures all things."
                                    - 1 Corinthians 13:7

CHAPTER IV. PEELING THE AGENT ORANGE

That day in August 1993 is a very difficult and painful day to recall. I remember looking out the backdoor window and watching Jim say good-bye to our three young children.

It is a visual I will never forget.

My twin sister, *Dianne*, my *Mother*, and her brother, my *Uncle Dan*, were arriving soon to assist me with the professional movers and help me pack up our mini-van for our final trip back to Georgia.

I so desperately wanted to ease this horrific transition which included the loss of our beautiful home, land, tree house, four Connemara (Irish) ponies, their close friends, Ricky and Spencer, and so much more – but most of all, *their Father.*

I had sold three of our ponies, and was having *Cricket* transported to Georgia with us as I felt having one of their ponies in Georgia would help my daughter, in particular. I had found a person who lived close to our new, and never seen, apartment who had a small pasture on which another pony resided. The owner agreed to a monthly boarding fee.

After a very grueling day, we finally finished packing my Uncle's car, our mini-van and the professional mover's truck.

As we drove away, I realized all I had to offer my children were the clothes on their backs and packed in boxes in the moving van, our dog, *Murphy*, a few rabbits in cages, *Cricket* the pony, an apartment we had never seen, schools they had never attended, friends they had not yet met, and memories......*lots and lots of memories.*

After we had traveled about forty-five minutes, my mini-van started making sounds that did not appear normal.

After they increased, they became a concern and all of us – except the professional movers. We turned into a full-service station where I asked the mechanic if he could determine what was wrong. I needed some reassurances that all was well.

As we sat on the curve in the hot sun, the mechanic walked over and took me to the side. He said, *"Lady, someone has poured paraffin into your gas tank!"* I said, *"What is "paraffin?"*

To which he responded, *"Wax."*

While I never sought confirmation, in my heart I knew what had happened – *and by whom.*

After sitting on the curve at the service station for six hours and paying nine hundred dollars in cash to the mechanic – almost all I had – I loaded our children into the van and we got back on the road to Georgia.

In 1994 – just one year after the children and I relocated to Georgia – I began having blurry vision and soon made an appointment for an eye checkup. I thought to myself, perhaps my prescription needed updating.

During the checkup, the eye doctor advised me that I would need to get an MRI *"STAT."*

A few days later, while preparing the children for dinner and bedtime, as it was a school night, I received a phone call from the Radiologist who said, *"You have a tumor wrapped around your optic nerve. You will need to have surgery as soon as possible."*

My response was, *"Surgery? I do not have time for surgery! I am raising three children on my own and working fulltime!"*

To which he replied, *"Mrs. Caldon. You do not understand. You have no choice. You have to make time."*

Shortly after that call, my family drove me to Atlanta where I underwent serious cranial surgery to remove the tumor – later determined to be Meningioma. While I was grateful to hear it was not cancerous, it was a major inconvenience!

When the Surgeon told me he would have to shave much of my hair, I laughed and said, *"You can't do that!"*

He responded with, *"You need to get your priorities straight."* To which I said, *"Every woman's hair is a "priority!"*

The normal recovery time for such surgeries is three months. I was back to work in five weeks. Only this time, I had to wear head bands as they did shave much of my hair.

I later learned from my secretary at the college, *Michelle*, that most of the campus community did not even know I had undergone surgery.

She said many of the campus community thought I was making a *"fashion statement"* with my matching head bands!

While the children and I had the last sixteen years to prepare and come to terms with Jim eventually being *"called home,"* the day I received the phone call at my college office, I realized.......***I was still not ready.***

Jim's sister – who had introduced us in 1979 – called to tell me Jim was not expected to live for another twenty-four hours.

I immediately left the office and picked up our children at their school. I remember explaining their Father was not doing well, and felt it best we be at home together if he passes away.

Jim had been living with the woman in Oregon since our separation in August of 1993.

85.

Sean expressed his strong desire to *"speak one last time to my Father,"* so I called Jim's hospital room. She, of course, answered the phone.

The response to Sean's repeated requests to speak to his dying Father one last time is best described by Sean, himself, in one of his two support letters submitted to the VA Claims System and a permanent part of our VA file at the Board of Veterans Appeals.

▪Excerpts from Sean's support letter dated 23 August 2007 submitted to the BVA:

"He (Jim) was to remain in a sterile environment for up to 6 months after the surgery. He was out in less than a few weeks. I was scared when I heard the news of his release, but remained silent. I wanted a quick recovery as much as anyone, but to rush him into a random apartment would serve no purpose."

"I know now the woman from Oregon (name withheld) moved Jim into the unsterile apartment for him to die. It was less than a week later that he (having no immune system) contacted the flue and died."

"The day my family became aware of this, was the same day that the woman from Oregon (name withheld) revealed herself for who she truly was. I grasped the phone listening to the woman who stands over my dying father. I asked her for one simple request. To hold the phone to his ear. Keep in mind I and the rest of my family are 3000 miles away. The woman from Oregon could have laid the phone on a table for all I care."

"It was the idea of maybe him hearing my voice before he died saying I love you. She abruptly said "no" and gave me multiple excuses as to why that was impossible. I pleaded with her to just put the phone by his ear. Each time I was denied this request."

My Husband of sixteen years, the Father of our three children, died on 17 July 1996. The children and I flew to Massachusetts for his funeral.

The Veterans Health Council states *"Agent Orange is a highly toxic herbicide used by the U.S. military during the Vietnam War to defoliate hiding places used by the enemy and to clear the perimeters of military installations."*

With Jim's record of service in the Navy Seabee's Mobile Construction Battalion, who were among the first to prepare areas for combat troops, on 24 September 1996, the VA released its Rating Decision regarding my Husband's death on 17 July 1996.

It states, in part: *"Prior to his death the veteran established service connection for non-Hodgkin's lymphoma due to herbicide exposure in Vietnam. Service connection for the cause of the veteran's death is granted since evidence shows that it was related to military service."*

Our children were now fifteen, fourteen and eleven years old. Realizing my sole responsibility for their upbringing, college, cars, medical insurance, food, housing, clothes, and more, I made an appointment at the local VA Services Office in downtown Macon. I needed to begin the paperwork for my VA DIC Spousal Benefits as soon as possible.

While I was in the VA Service Office, I was informed… *the woman from Oregon had already filed for my VA DIC Spousal Benefits earlier and was receiving my VA Benefits already.*

I was stunned and in total disbelief. *This could not possibly be true.*

We were married for sixteen years and had three children. ***They were never married, had no children and she was receiving my monthly VA DIC Spousal Benefits?***

I immediately thought to myself,

"How could the VA make such an egregious mistake in judgment?!"

I had done some research and, according to the **VA Chapter 2: Surviving Members of Vietnam Veterans Who Have Died** *"Self-Help Guide on Agent Orange,"* the surviving family member entitled to DIC *"must satisfy the first of the two requirements for DIC, you must be able to show the VA that you are one of the following types of surviving family members:"*

"....you were married to the veteran at the time of death, and you lived continuously with the veteran from the date you were married until the veteran's death, unless separation occurred due to the veteran's misconduct without fault on your part, and you are currently not married."

When I first brought this person's fraudulent submission of the VA DIC Spousal Benefits Application to the attention of the VA Regional Office in Portland, Oregon in 1996, their response to me was:

"We have too many cases similar to yours. We do not get involved. You will have to fight your VA Claim with a private attorney."

Unlike the requirements mandated by the Social Security Administration nationwide, *the VA Claims System did not even bother to verify the validity of this woman from Oregon's fraudulent VA DIC Spousal Application.*

A few years later, I began dating a person I did not know very well. We later married – which lasted less than one year. This was a failed attempt on my part to try and provide my three young teenagers the *"white picket fence"* and some normalcy – as they had not known either for a long time.

It was during this time I realized, in order, to obtain a marriage license, I would need a certified one of mine and Jim's marriage certificate as I only had a copy.

And, with the fact I was never notified of any official divorce proceedings, and with the woman from Oregon succeeding in scamming the VA and also getting my Husband to change his Will shortly before his death, I felt I needed to confirm what our legal status was.

I had never signed or seen any divorce papers. I was too busy putting food on the table and working fulltime. I never had the time or energy to confirm the legalities of what I was being told by the woman from Oregon.

During this research, I learned the woman from Oregon had submitted a fraudulent divorce decree for me and my Husband with her VA DIC Spousal Benefits Application. Again, *a document I had never seen or been notified was being filed.*

When I finally obtained a copy of the fraudulent divorce decree, it was dated **6 May 1996** – *only 72 days before my husband's death on 17 July 1996* – and during the time frame he had been classified as *"fully disabled."*

Common sense dictates these close dates should have been a *"red flag"* to someone at the VA Portland Oregon Regional Office.

The fact her and my Husband's fraudulent marriage certificate – which she also submitted with her VA DIC Spousal Benefits Application - *was dated 8 July 1994 -* **almost two years BEFORE the fraudulent divorce decree** – *dated 6 May 1996* - **should have been another "red flag" to the VA!**

When I brought the official VA ruling for VA-Certified Agent Orange Deceased Victims' Spousal Benefits, which states:

"...spousal benefits are granted if separation occurred due to the veteran's misconduct without fault on your part....," to the attention of the VA Claims Representative in Atlanta, *he acted like he did not even know to what I was referring!*

I later obtained a copy of the woman from Oregon's official VA DIC Spousal Benefits Application. I reported the fact she had submitted false dates on her VA DIC Spousal Application – a federal form - to the **VA Fraud Hot Line**.

The VA Fraud Hot Line never responded.

When I brought this falsification of a federal document to the attention of the VA Claims Representatives in both the VA Regional Offices in Atlanta and Portland, they, too, were not interested.

I have the names and contact information of all the VA Claims Representatives in the VA Regional Offices in Atlanta and Portland with whom I have corresponded for over eighteen years – and, more recently, in the TN VA Regional Office.

Our separation was on record and commonly known throughout the family due to an unstable home environment – later described in a Medical Assessment as *"severe psychiatric decompensation which lasted until the end of his life."*

I was working full-time in the Office of the President of a public college (now Middle Georgia State University), raising three children, and completing a vast amount of VA paperwork to correct the VA's blatant error.

Little did I know, I would be still filling out VA forms, attending hearings, and waiting *"90 more days"* for resolution for the next nineteen years while the woman from Oregon received my VA DIC Spousal Benefits every month since my Husband's death in July 1996.

The horrific circumstances which resulted in my three young children and I being forced to relocate to Georgia in August 1993 have been detailed and confirmed repeatedly in medical assessments, support letters and documents submitted to the Georgia VA Regional Office in Atlanta for now nineteen years, Briefs to the Board of Veterans Appeals, Hearing on 8 April 2008 in Washington, D.C. and the U S. Court of Appeals for Veterans Claims. The VA does not care about the truth and sacrifices our family has made and continues to make. We are just a file number.

It is now November 2015, and the VA continues to "stall, deny and hope I die."

In 2000, I was invited to attend my 30th High School Miller/Lanier Reunion and, at the last minute, decided to attend. A few weeks before the big event, I received a phone call from Richard (a.k.a. *"Ebbie"*). He and I had dated in high school.

He said he had seen on the RSVP list I would be attending and asked if I be interested in going out with him the night before. I said, *"Yes."*

It was a wonderful *"reunion"* for many reasons.

Richard and I dated for six months. He asked me to marry him. He lived in Tallahassee, Florida and we were making plans for him to relocate to Macon soon. Our being together, as he had two young sons, brought me a glimmer of hope for a brighter future for my family....*one we had not shared for some time.*

In March 2001, I drove down to Tallahassee to visit Richard only to be greeted at his home by police cars, his two sons, his friends and family.

Richard had been killed a few hours earlier while returning home from the golf course. I was in shock.

Death, again, had caught me completely by surprise.

I offered my condolences to his children and returned to my car. The drive home alone was very difficult as I could not see the road for the tears.

I called my friend, Gay. I called my sister, Janie. She and her, now late, Husband, Ed, immediately drove from their home in Albany, Georgia. They caught up with me half-way back to Macon. They did not want me to drive back home under these unexpected circumstances alone.

Again, *GOD simply had other plans….*

Our Daily Reminder….

"Death leaves a heartache no one can heal, love leaves a memory no one can steal."
> - From a headstone in Ireland

CHAPTER V. BLESS THE BROKEN ROAD

Just like the song, *The Impossible Dream*, when I first heard a childhood friend, *Buddy Greene*, now in Nashville, TN, sing the song, **"Bless the Broken Road,"** (made famous by Rascal Flatts), I knew immediately the lyrics were describing not only my life, but the lives of so many Veterans and their families.

The lyrics remind us......

> *GOD blessed the broken road*
> *That led me straight to you....*
> *It's all part of a grander plan –*
> *That is coming true."*

Because of the VA's critical need for re-organization, Veterans and their families simply have to travel many *"broken roads"* to get there.

Having lost *Jim* to cancer, and both my younger brother, *Craig*, and my high school boyfriend and fiancé, *Richard*, in car accidents, I was not taking the dating life too seriously.

While the opportunities were there, my heart was simply not. *It was still mending.*

I was soon to learn, *again*, GOD had his own agenda.

The local churches had begun a monthly *"Christian Singles"* event just down the street from our home, but the thought was far too depressing to consider – even with the fact my twin sister, *Dianne*, had met her Husband, *Ron*, there and they were very happy.

A divorced friend of mine wanted very much to attend this monthly event, and encouraged me to attend with her.

I finally agreed to walk her in the door, to lessen her anxiety, but, told her emphatically, *"I am not staying!"*

As soon as I entered The Cupola, where the event was taking place, I wanted to turn around and go home. I was getting too old for the *"Dating Game!"*

A short while later, as I was saying my good-byes, I glanced across to a table. There sat a gentleman all by himself. He clearly had my attention. As a casual friend, *Mike*, walked by, I asked him to ask this person if he would like to dance with me. I certainly was not going to ask him myself.

That was thirteen years ago.

Randy and I have since traveled many *"broken roads"* together. Most have been wonderful. However, because of my continued battle with the VA, many of our roads were, at times, *very bumpy.*

In January 2003, when our youngest son, *Bryan*, turned eighteen, he asked his brother, *Sean*, and his sister, *Logan*, to skydive with him to *"celebrate"* what our family had overcome physically, emotionally and financially during and following their Father's long illness.

It was a very symbolic day. *Ed Grisamore,* Columinst for The Macon Telegraph, featured an article in our local newspaper in which he said....

"When she asked why they wanted to do something so daring, they said they wanted to celebrate what they had been through to become a close-knit family. Six years ago, her husband, Jim, died after a long battle with non-Hodgkin's lymphoma.

"They are all incredible young people who have beaten the odds through determination, perseverance and spirit," Denise said. *"(They have) a passion for life, as they know first-hand how easily it can be taken away."*

SEAN

LOGAN

BRYAN

104.

I also received an unexpected call that year from my daughter's college sweetheart. I had friends over for dinner, so I took the call in my bedroom. He asked for my daughter's hand in marriage! I cried with joy! I had to promise not to tell anyone as he was planning to *"pop the question"* on an upcoming trip and after he had purchased an engagement ring.

I asked him if he would like to consider giving Logan the engagement ring given to me by her Father - once worn by Logan's Grandmother's, *Jim's Mother*. He immediately accepted. He had it reset beautifully.

Logan and her college sweetheart were married at *Christopher's Place* in Newport, Tennessee. Our sons, Sean and Bryan, walked Logan down the aisle in honor of their Father.

I had an empty chair with roses placed near the front during the service in Jim's memory – *my late Husband...their Father.*

Our youngest son, Bryan, was completing high school graduation from First Presbyterian Day School in 2003. I had already completed the paperwork for him to attend Valdosta State – as his sister had – and paid the initial fees for his dorm.

Bryan asked me to sit down one afternoon as he wanted to tell me something. *He informed me he had been accepted into the Navy.* He would be entering the Nuclear Engineering Program as soon as he graduated from high school.

After I got over the initial shock, as I had no idea of his plans, I congratulated him. I thought to myself, at least he would not be fighting in the jungles and getting riddled with herbicide like his Father.

His Father would be so proud.......as I was.

Our family flew to Illinois for Bryan's Boot Camp graduation. It was a very exciting event and a stadium full of brave new soldiers and their families. When we departed, each graduating new Navy student were told to proceed to get their final *"to go"* home paperwork. It was only a few days before Christmas, and we were on cloud nine!

Little did we know, it would be another *"adventure"* in our family's journey together!

We waited and waited and waited. *No Bryan*.

Finally, a Navy personnel officer informed me the Navy Officer in charge of releasing special recruits – in this case, the Nuclear Engineer recruits – had departed for the holidays immediately after the ceremony.

Bryan did not have the proper paperwork to fly home!

"What!!???" Say that again. *My son was going to sit in a another state, with no family at Christmas because someone forgot to sign the proper paperwork?*

GOD help us.....*it sounded far too familiar!*

And, me, Bryan's Mother - who had been fighting the VA for years - was going to simply walk graciously with the rest of the family, fly home and leave my young son?

They clearly did not know me very well.

The repeated response from the family members in Illinois with me was, *"Do not get involved. This will work itself out."*

For the next four to five hours we sat in a local fast food chain.

We were barely speaking.

After five hours passed, and with the realization our flight would be leaving soon, one of the family members said, *"Mom, get involved!"*

That was all I needed. I proceeded to the nearest Navy official's desk and began pleading with the Navy officials still there – as many had immediately departed for Christmas following the ceremony!

About one hour later, **Bryan appeared!** With the signed paperwork finally in hand, off we went to the airport! We had very little time to get there.

When we arrived at the Delta check-in counter, I remember telling the Delta representative our story. I asked her to let someone know why we were late arriving as we only had minutes to get through the Security and board our plane – which was scheduled to depart in less than ten minutes!

When we boarded the plane soon after, we were greeted with applause!!! *The pilot had held the plane for us!*

Yes, GOD is good.....very, very good. And, that day, *so were the personnel and pilots of Delta Airlines!*

In November of 2004, I began losing my balance. When my vision was not what it should be, I felt, perhaps, it was time to have another MRI – given I had surgery in 1994 for the same symptoms – which resulted in major surgery.

I was told that my meningioma was back.

I returned to Emory Hospital again and had the same major surgery I had in 1994. Only this time *Dr. Jeffrey Olson* required me to follow up with radiation for six weeks – which I did.

I drove to the hospital located downtown during my lunch hour each day to receive my radiation treatments while working fulltime in the Office of a University System of Georgia College President, providing financial resources for two children in college, and filed more paperwork for my VA DIC Spousal Benefits when I could.

My radiologist, *Dr. Drew Cole*, advised me to *"buy stocks in MRIs."* While I have not bought any stocks in MRIs, I do have annual MRIs - as he encouraged.

So far, all is well.

Through two major surgeries, the deaths of many close to my heart, and my never ending battle with the VA, I came to appreciate the precious gifts in life money cannot buy.

As it is said often, every day is a *"gift"* – and one most people open each day and throw away as if another will be given to them tomorrow.

Sadly, I have learned, firsthand, *this is not always true.*

Our Daily Reminders….

"When you're down to nothing, GOD is up to something. The faithful see the invisible, believe the incredible and then receive….
the "impossible."   - Author Unknown

"Miracles often arrive at the moment we depart from fear and head toward faith."
                              - Small Miracles for Women

CHAPTER VI.
"STALL, DENY AND HOPE THEY DIE" – THE VA'S UNWRITTEN POLICY

After my Husband's death and after years of denials to my VA DIC Spousal Benefits Claims, I was encouraged by the VA Services representative in Macon, *Roger Freeman*, to obtain more medical assessments.

I was hesitant to call my brother, *Jimmy*, a Board Certified Medical Oncologist, who had consulted in my Husband's case with the oncologists in Chapel Hill, as I realized how busy his oncology practice was in Georgia and I also realized it is difficult for oncologists to consult when it is a family member.

I did, finally, call Jimmy. Later that afternoon, I heard a knock on my front door. My brother handed me his medical assessment letter. I cried when I read it as he had put his heart into his medical assessment.

I have shared with you some of the excerpts from his medical assessment as well for you to better understand what the children and I faced during a very difficult time. Not only were we preparing for their Father's ultimate death, but we had the horrific experience of watching him slowly die in front of us for many years.

I remember years of crying in disbelief as the children and I tried, with much difficulty, to live our daily routines, while preparing for the inevitable – *Jim's death.*

My brother, *Dr. James F. Smith, Jr.*, again, a Board Certified Medical Oncologist, stated in his Medical Assessment, in part, ***"his decline psychologically was precipitated by the diagnosis, exacerbated severely by the Interferon, and further promulgated by the progressive disease with a known fatal outcome predicted at the outset. All of this led to a severe psychiatric decompensation which lasted until the end of his life."***

He also pointed out in his medical assessment:

"This was a tragedy on multiple levels, not only in the loss of a young, intelligent man, but in the severe repercussions that his depression had on his lovely wife and his young children."

Medical assessments were also submitted by *Stephen A. Bernard, MD, FACP,* one of Jim's Oncologists at the NC Memorial Hospital, and *Kathryn S. Kolibaba, M.D., Oncologist* with the Oregon Health Sciences University.

Even with the detailed medical assessments in hand, the VA continues to avoid addressing the facts sitting on their desks for now nineteen years.

In the Summer of 2007, after paying, for me, a large amount of legal fees and a plane fare for our oldest son, *Sean*, to fly in from California, he and I attended a court Hearing together in Chapel Hill, NC at which my Attorney, *Lisa Wagner*, requested the court to void the fraudulent divorce decree strongly believed to have been filed on 6 May 1996 – *just 72 days before my Husband of sixteen years' death on 17 July 1996 and during which he was on his death bed* – by the woman from Oregon.

This person from Oregon – who was never married to my Husband and who has received my VA DIC Spousal Benefits for now nineteen years – did not even attend the Hearing.

The Judge denied our request.

During our trip to Chapel Hill for the Hearing, my oldest son, Sean, and I drove out to our former home.

While it was a very sentimental and, at moments, an emotional visit, as we drove away we both agreed the family home we built together for over ten years no longer existed. *It was gone.*

Chapel Hill Attorney, *Lisa Wagner*, knew that my financial abilities to appeal the ruling would be difficult. She graciously informed me that she would be submitting an Appeal to the North Carolina Court of Appeals on my behalf.

Needless to say, *I was, elated!*

Attorney Lisa Wagner will always be my "Guardian Angel." She stepped up to a very difficult plate during a very arduous time. **She is one of the individuals who believed in our family, made a true difference and to whom I will be forever grateful.**

During this time, Randy and I were going through many difficult challenges following the loss of my twenty-year college career and financial struggles.

I was looking for a new church home and was encouraged to attend Martha Bowman United Methodist Church.

The first time I visited *Martha Bowman United Methodist Church*, the warmth from the members – members I did not even know – was like a comforting and warm blanket.

While I knew during the years since my Husband's terminal illness diagnosis, GOD was *"listening"* to me, as I had reached out to him often, it was not until the sermon that day by Pastor Bob Moon did I finally realize, *"I was not listening to GOD*

During Pastor Bob Moon's sermon that morning, I felt strongly that he was talking directly to me.

I was finally listening.

Pastor Bob held up a sailboat and said, *"God's wind will continue to help you sail....but you must cut your anchors."*

This incredible sermon from Pastor Bob Moon changed my life – and I have not looked back. A few months later, I gave a Testimony at this church and mentioned the significance of the sailboat that Pastor Bob Moon had mentioned in his sermon.

A few weeks after my Testimony, I opened my mailbox and found a beautiful wooden and bronze sailboat by members of the Church I had never met. It is in our home today with one of my favorite scriptures printed on the sail, which reminds me of one of my favorites......

OUR DAILY REMINDER....

"A ship is safe in harbor, but that's not what ships are for."
— William Shedd

On 12 September 2006, I filed an official Appeal to the *Board of Veterans Appeals*. This was *"pro se."* In other words, I had no legal representation for this major legal step. While working full-time, filing college scholarships and adding major debt to my credit cards – including a second mortgage on our home, to which Randy graciously co-signed, I researched the legalities and filed it myself.

I had always had a passion for the legal field. I had even gone back to school and obtained an associate degree in Criminal Justice a few years earlier – in my *"spare time"* from my full-time job in the Office of the President at the local college.

Our daughter, Logan, and her husband, welcomed their first child in October 2007 – *a girl!* Randy and I flew to Texas just in time and were there to greet her into our lives.

My granddaughter's very existence built even more determination on my part to have the VA *"right this wrong"* as my children and grandchildren (now five) are paying the price of the VA's mistake as well as I cannot afford to do what most Grandmothers do. I cannot visit them often due to the financial costs.

In April 2008, I flew to Washington, D.C. and had a hearing before the Board of Veterans Appeals.

Prior to the hearing, a DAV Representative (I *prefer not to disclose his name)* reviewed my file, attended the Board of Veterans Appeals Hearing with me in Washington, and stated to me:

"The VA Regional Office in Atlanta really dropped the ball in your Claim. They made a very big mistake. With my experience, it is my strong guess the VA will never admit it."

As we walked down the hall to the Hearing, he further stated to me:

"You do know what the VA's unwritten policy is, don't you?"

I responded, *"No."*

He then said….

"The VA's unwritten policy is, "STALL, DENY AND HOPE THEY DIE."

Unfortunately, the BVA hearing in Washington, D.C. – of which I had worked to have happen for over a decade - was very much routine and *"uneventful."* The questions were generic in nature. The vast amount of physical evidence, Medical Assessments and even the "Emo-Sphere" I brought to the Hearing with me were **never discussed or even mentioned by the BVA Judge.**

In Chapel Hill, my Husband spent thousands of dollars (that we did not have) on gold leaf paint. He would sit at the kitchen counter for hours before and after his chemotherapy treatments in our new home painting Styrofoam balls with the gold leaf. He called them *"Emo-Spheres."*

Jim told our three young children his would be *"selling his new invention to Hallmark"* and it would *"ensure their financial future"* upon his death.

The description below was written by Jim:

Emo-Sphere

The beauty of Emo-Sphere is the tangible representation of your commitment and vulnerability to another and is a visible sign on how well the relationship is doing.

Emo-Sphere is covered in gold, it is divided in such a way that each may claim half of the sphere as their own.

During the course of your relationship the pain and hurt that is experienced can be shown by defacing, in someway, this representation of your relationship. This defacing is to be on your side only. This allows your partner to visualize the damage to the relationship and is a reminder of the pain experienced.

Patent Pending

Upon leaving our home of thirteen years in August of 1993 – which we lost to foreclosure – I found over twenty of these Styrofoam balls - painted in gold leaf by my Husband - in our barn.

The critical fact submitted to the BVA Judge by *Lisa Wagner*, Chapel Hill Attorney, that she had filed an appeal to the North Carolina Court of Appeals requesting the ruling by the NC Judge be remanded – which brought into question the validity of the fraudulent divorce decree filed by the woman from Oregon - did not appear to be of any importance to the BVA judge overseeing the Hearing.

Even with all the new evidence and medical assessments and pending ruling from the N.C. Court of Appeals on the fraudulent divorce decree, **on 22 July 2008, following the Board of Veterans Appeals hearing in Washington, D.C., *I received in the mail another denial to my years of claims for VA DIC Spousal Benefits.***

The DAV Representative at the Washington, D.C. Hearing was right – my struggle to have the BVA address accountability of VA Regional Offices in both Portland, OR and Atlanta, GA – and, years later, Nashville, TN – would be an uphill battle. I will continue climbing "uphill" for as long as it takes – and not just for me – but, for all Veterans and their families.

On 24 September 2008, after fifteen years in the Office of the President at Middle Georgia State College (formerly Macon State College) – following my submitting in writing the concerns I had verbalized for years regarding the President's requests to cross ethical, fiscal and, what is now being investigated, criminal lines – *I was terminated.*

The facts confirmed very serious malfeasance within Georgia's higher education system by officials at the *Board of Regents of the University System of Georgia* that negatively impact Georgia families from over thirty public colleges.

The facts in my subsequent Whistleblower lawsuit are known by Georgia's Governor, *Nathan Deal,* and top attorney, *Attorney General Sam Olens* – who authorized the filing of four oppositions in Fulton County Superior Court in his continued efforts to keep the evidence confirming malfeasance sealed from public view. Georgia's reputation for being one of the most corrupt state governments in the nation has, sadly, become the norm and one our General Assembly refuses to address.

While Atlanta Attorney, *Chris Moorman,* Political Vine Editor/Publisher, *Bill Simon,* and Athens Attorney, *Stephen F. Humphreys,* attempted diligently to have the state's court system address the evidence of malfeasance detailed in my Whistleblower case, and an increasing number of other lawsuits, the infamous influence of Georgia's *"good 'ole boy network"* (a.k.a. *"The Untouchables"*) prevails – for now. Attorney Humphreys requested Georgia Governor Nathan Deal to appoint a Special Investigator three times – *to which Governor Deal would not respond.*

The sudden loss of my two decade college career (*I formerly worked with the Chancellor at UNC-Chapel Hill and a Vice President at Mercer University*) was another *"life changing"* event which made by long and difficult battle with the VA Claims System even more stressful.

Our oldest son, Sean, was now living back at home during his recent return home from California. For him, I needed to stay strong.

On a positive note, on 2 December 2008, just two months after losing my job in the Office of the President of a public college for objecting to criminal malfeasance, I was waiting in the Social Security Office in Macon, GA. I noticed I had missed a call from my Chapel Hill, NC attorney, *Lisa Wagner.*

When I listened to her voice message, *I cried.*

Ms. Wagner had called to tell me the North Carolina Court of Appeals had ruled the fraudulent divorce decree – allegedly filed by the person in Oregon – was "Void!"

Finally, perhaps now, the VA Claims System will make right their blatant mistake and absence of legal judgment that made the loss of my Husband and my children's Father even more painful for so many years.

I was wrong – very wrong.

In 2009, after much research, I obtained the services of *Bergmann and Moore, LLC Attorney firm from Bethesda, MD.* Their reputation was very encouraging and, after speaking with *Ms. Liz Robbins*, a VA Case Manager, I was encouraged even more.

She explained the firm, while concerned and addressed the emotional toll of each Veteran and their family member, their primary objective in each case was the legal basis to be brought before the Board of Veterans Appeals in Washington, D.C.

My VA DIC Spousal Claim was black and white – not gray.

With the fact I had no financial source to offer *Bergmann and Moore* a retainer fee, they agreed to a contingency agreement as they felt very confident in the legal standing of my individual battle with the VA.

With my higher education career Retirement Fund almost depleted, following the loss of my college career, Randy assisted my keeping the lights on in the home I had purchased one year before we met in 2001.

This financial stress – along with my years battling the VA Claims System - contributed greatly to our *"on and off"* again relationship.

We had talked about getting married earlier, but the VA has a policy that if you marry before the age of fifty-seven, **even if you lose your Husband from a service-related death like I did,** you are not eligible for VA DIC Spousal Benefits.

In other words....*"You can lose your Husband, the Father of your children, while he is serving and protecting our Nation's freedom, but you cannot remarry until you are close to being a senior!"*

Excuse me for asking, but, *"What man created that mandate?"*

In July 2009, Randy purchased airfare for us to fly to Texas for the birth of my daughter and her husband's second child - *a son.*

It was times like these, when GOD opened another door and brought so much joy into my life, I found the energy and determination to keep fighting my long battle with the VA.   133.

The fact the VA was closing the doors the minute one was slightly opened was not going to stop me.

I realized the VA's unwritten policy of ***"Stall, Deny and Hope They Die"*** may become a reality for me – given my meningioma surgeries in 1994 and 2004, but I had children and grandchildren who deserved the VA's attention. For them, I was not going away.

On 24 May 2010, *Bergmann and Moore, LLC* law firm submitted an Appeal to the U. S. Court of Appeals for Veterans Claims in Washington, D.C. This time the Brief documented the final ruling from the North Carolina Court of Appeals - dated 2 December 2008 - which confirmed the fraudulent divorce 6 May 1996 decree – ***filed just 72 days prior to my Husband's death and allegedly orchestrated by the woman from Oregon*** – was, indeed, **"Void."**

My Husband of sixteen years and this woman from Oregon were never married.

Bergmann and Moore later discovered (through their request allowed by the *Freedom of Information Act)* correspondence to this woman from Oregon from the VA Portland Regional Office in which they did, indeed, question the validity of the documents she had submitted with her VA DIC Spousal Benefits Application in 1996. Yet, the VA allowed her fraudulent VA DIC Spousal Benefits Application to be approved – *even without a legitimate marriage certificate!*

As the DAV Representative stated at my Hearing in Washington, D.C. in 2008, *"The VA dropped the ball. They will never admit this mistake."*

On 8 September 2010, my VA attorney from *Bergmann and Moore* called and said, *"We just received notice that the U. S. Court of Appeals for Veterans Claims in Washington, D.C. has ruled for a "Joint Motion for an Order Vacating and Remanding the Board Decision and Incorporating the Terms of this Remand."*

In other words, the U. S. Court of Appeals for Veterans Claims *"vacated and remanded"* the Board of Veterans Appeals' 22 July 2008 Denial of my VA DIC Spousal Benefits Claims!

My attorney further stated receiving a **"Joint Motion for Remand"** from the VA's top court in Washington, D.C. is *"very rare."*

The actual statement on page four of the Joint Motion from the U. S. Court of Appeals for Veterans Claims states, in part:

"WHEREFORE, the parties respectfully move the Court for an order vacating and remanding the July 22, 2008, Board decision."

This 2010 Joint Motion further ruled,
"Finally, the Board must provide expedited treatment of this case under 38 U.S.C. § 7112."

My Family's story is one example of the VA Claims System's non-compliance to **"expedited treatment"** ruled by the U. S. Court of Appeals for Veterans Claims.

I have submitted requests to elected officials and Chairmen of U.S. Senate and House VA Committees for over ten years and asked for their assistance in scheduling me to speak before any VA Committee – anywhere, anytime. Among them are: *Georgia Senator Johnny Isakson* – a member of the U.S. Senate VA Committee (R–GA), *recently appointed Chairman*, *U.S. Congressman Scott DesJarlais* (R-TN), *Senator Janice Bowling*, (R-TN), *U.S. Representative Austin Scott* (R-GA), and even *President Barack Obama, The White House (D)*.

I have received no response regarding my speaking requests from Chairman Johnny Isakson. My requests to speak before Georgia and U.S. Senate and House VA Committees continue.

I would ask each VA Committee member to put themselves in my position for one moment and ask themselves.....

"What would you do if, after losing your spouse of sixteen years – the Father of your three children - from a "service-related death" you learned the VA was paying your VA DIC Spousal Benefits to an individual who was never married to your Spouse, has no children, and who knowingly submitted false information on a VA DIC Spousal Benefits Application?"

"Would you simply walk away after nineteen years of making economic, physical and emotional sacrifices as a Veterans Widow and single parent of three young children – which included the loss of two homes to foreclosure, bankruptcy and countless trips to pawn shops to put food on the table for dinner?"

Given they are lawmakers and members of Veterans Affairs Committees, I would ask:

138.

"Why are VA Applications and documents not given the same scrutiny and verification required by the Social Security Administration?"

"Who enforces compliance by the State VA Regional Offices following Motions for Remands by both the Board of Veteran Affairs and the U. S. Court of Appeals for Veterans Claims in Washington, D.C.?"

As I mentioned in my Introduction, years ago I was asked to write a speech about a government agency for a baccalaureate speech class.

I chose the Veterans Administration.

As the Professor requested, I began my speech with statistics and numbers. Then I closed my notes, paused and stated to the class......

"If you remember just one thing from my speech tonight, please keep in mind that the file number in each case you will work on in public agencies are not just numbers. File numbers represent 'real people'......'real families.'

My family is one of those families."

I then took the cover off a large framed photo of our family that was on a podium beside me – *the photo I mentioned earlier my Husband wanted taken just one month after my husband was diagnosed on 27 January 1987 with terminal cancer.*

I, then, introduced myself to the class and told them our family's VA story and how broken the VA Claims System was for so many Veterans and their families like ours.

The students in the class were listening – *unlike the VA Claims System for now nineteen years.* There were many tears shed that night and not just from me. I received an "A."

During one of my frequent visits to the Atlanta VA Regional Office, I was asked by one of the Claims Representative, *Mary Love*, for a copy of my speech on the VA.

I assumed she was going to share it with her colleagues. I would not know as I rarely heard from this VA Claims Representative or *Herbert Ward, Claims Counselor*, who I was told was overseeing my Claim. I lost count of the very personal and pleading conversations with both Ms. Love and Mr. Ward in which I begged for their assistance – to no avail.

In 2009, I also requested a copy of my BVA file. When it arrived, it was quite large.

As I was reviewing the documents, I suddenly noticed that the last BVA status of *my VA Claim update – addressed to me* – dated 30 December 2008 – **had been mailed by the BVA Director of Management and Administration to the address of the woman in Oregon -** *the very person never married to my Husband, who falsified a VA DIC Spousal Benefits Application in 1996 following the death of my Husband of sixteen years (the Father of our three children) and to whom the VA has paid over $238,000 of my VA DIC Spousal Benefits!*

Besides my complete anger, disbelief and utter frustration, I could not help but note - ***"This is not "rocket science!***

Is the VA making these serious errors in the files of other Veterans and their family members?"

GOD help us...

I immediately brought this major breach of confidentiality to the BVA's attention by contacting *Don Ewalt,* Constituent Representative of Senator Johnny Isakson – again, a member of the U.S. Senate VA Committee for many years who was appointed Chairman of the Senate Committee on Veterans' Affairs 7 January 2015, and *Debbie Blankenship,* Constituent Representative for former Representative Jim Marshall.

On 20 May 2009, I received a personal apology letter from *Margaret L. Peak,* FOIA (Freedom of Information Act), Privacy Act Officer with the BVA. I later received copies of apology letters from *Chairman of the Board of Veterans Appeals, James P. Terry,* sent to former *Representative Jim Marshall* and *Senator Johnny Isakson.*

BVA Chairman James P. Terry, said in his apology to Senator Johnny Isakson, in part:

143.

"On December 30, 2008, the Board forwarded a letter to Ms. Caldon regarding the status of her claim. The fact that the information was received by another appellant was done in error and constitutes a breach of Ms. Caldon's privacy. We humbly apologize for this error and a letter of apology has been written to Ms. Caldon. The address correction has been made and our records have been updated to reflect the correction.

The Board takes its responsibility to protect the private information of veterans and their dependents very seriously. We deeply regret that this situation occurred and are reviewing our policies and practices to ensure that every possible precaution is taken to keep this from happening again."

My hundreds of emails and pleads for assistance to the VA continued between my working part-time jobs and depleting my college retirement fund for routine living expenses and attorney fees.

After the loss of my twenty-year higher education career for objecting to criminal malfeasance by officials in Georgia's higher education system – commonly known throughout the campuses as the *"Southern Mafia"* - *Jeff Chirico, CBS46,* brought his news team to my home and interviewed me in November 2013:
http://www.cbsatlanta.com/story/23973296/former-employee-board-of-regents-hiding-records

In March of 2011, Randy and I, Sean, Logan and her two children attended the wedding of our youngest son, *Bryan,* and *Ali.* Bryan had met Ali at a church he was visiting following his return home from deployment.

We were thrilled to finally meet Ali's family. We found everything we had heard about her wonderful family to be true.

Her Father, *Stephen,* also a Veteran, her siblings and family are of strong faith and values.

For a time, our family's focus during their wedding festivities was on creating new memories - not just remembering and living with the ones from which we were, in many ways, still recovering.

A short time later, our daughter, *Logan*, and her husband announced they were expecting their third child. I could not help but remember the similar scenario Logan's Father and I had in Chapel Hill – *being pregnant every two years!*

In January 2012, their second son arrived. Our daughter now had a daughter and two sons - *just like her Father and I had* – before we learned Agent Orange and the VA Claims System would play major roles in trying to destroy our Family's dreams....

Even with the indifference and incompetence of the VA and the unquestionable criminal malfeasance by Georgia's higher education officials at the **Board of Regents of the University System of Georgia,** *ignored by Governor Nathan Deal and not investigated by Georgia's Attorney General Sam Olens*, I will always stay strong for Randy, my children, my beautiful grandchildren and all Veterans and their families.

Looking back, the lives of our three young children and me had been a *"carousel"* with highs and lows for many years. Following years of watching my children's Father slowly slip away, I was at a mall in Chapel Hill one day when I came across a portrait of three beautiful ponies on a carousel.

I immediately felt that the visual was a reflection of the lives of our three young children with the *"ups and downs"* we were experiencing on now, a daily basis. With the fact it was three ponies – like the ones we had at our country home - I knew this portrait was meant for our family to have! *It has been hung in our home ever since and brings back reminders each time I walk by of the journey our family has walked together........*

OUR DAILY REMINDER....

"And who is there to harm you if you prove zealous for what is good? But even if you should suffer for the sake of righteousness, you are blessed."
                                             - 1 Peter 3:13-17

CHAPTER VII: TENNESSEE DETOUR

In August of 2012, with the financial and emotional toll following the loss of my fifteen-year position in the Office of the President at Middle Georgia State College and no resolution from the VA, I had no choice but to turn in the keys to the home my children and I lived in for the past twelve years.

Just like our *"Camelot"* home in Chapel Hill, North Carolina during my husband's terminal illness, *our family home in Georgia was lost to foreclosure. My filing bankruptcy followed.*

149.

These increasing and, at times, insurmountable events and uphill battles took a dramatic toll on my ten-year relationship with Randy. We decided to go our separate ways.

I moved to Tennessee to be closer to assist my daughter and her three young children as she was addressing concerns that needed her immediate attention.

I had my VA file transferred to the TN VA Regional Office in Nashville. During my year in Tennessee, I was introduced to *Iris Rudder*, Chairman, of the Franklin County Republican Party. Iris introduced me to *Congressman Scott DeJaslais*, R-District,, whose Constituent Services/Field Representative, *Isiah Robinson*, was among the few in Tennessee who truly cared and listened.

I attended The Franklin County Republican Party's Town Hall meeting on 23 February 2013 to simply introduce myself to three elected officials in hopes that they would assist in my repeated requests to speak before VA Affairs Committees both in Tennessee and Washington, D.C.

During the "Q&A" session, one of the attendees mentioned the VA. I suddenly found myself at the podium in front of a microphone in front of an audience of a room full of people – with no notes – to talk about the VA. I found my message came easily as my family's story is embedded in my mind and heart.

I simply offered the three elected officials my time and energy to speak whenever and as often as possible – on behalf of all Veterans and their families. I gave a very brief summary of my family's long battle with the VA Claims System.

As I departed the podium, I looked up and, to my complete surprise, *found everyone in the room offering a standing ovation, cheering me on and offering genuine applause...!*

That pivotal moment in my nineteen-year battle with the VA's Claims System will remain in my heart forever – another catalyst for me to continue a "mission" that GOD asked me to take on so many years ago.

Many Veterans and their family members introduced themselves to me after the meeting in which they expressed, they, too, had experienced the same indifference from the VA Claims System and, in most cases, had simply given up.

As the DAV Representative in Washington said stated to me, this is what the VA Claims System wants Veterans and their family members to do – ***give up.*** And, with the VA stalling long enough – *many Veterans and their families do.*

The Veterans Administration's **failure** to verify applications and fraudulent documents submitted, total disregard for documents confirming the facts, lack of education by VA Claims representatives on the laws, and non-compliance to rulings by the Board of Veterans Appeals and the U. S. Court of Appeals for Veterans Claims in Washington, D.C. represent our Country's increasing national disgrace and indifference to the sacrifices so many Veterans and their families have made for our Country's freedom.

Again, *my family is one example of many.*

I became a member of *Monteagle Memorial Methodist Church.* The owners of the cottage, which I was renting, were long time members there as well.....*Richard and Peggy Partin.* They welcomed me into their church and home at a time when I needed them more than they knew.

We became dear friends.

153.

The congregation has a wonderful history of community outreach to those in need and once a month they offer food to the needy. I recall one Saturday volunteering alongside many of my fellow parishioners.

As I assisted filling the bags up for those in line, I remember thinking, I wish I could ask for help as I had very little in the cottage. My pride would not let me ask them or my daughter's family. The Pawn Shop in Winchester – just *"down the mountain"* as I was told is the proper way to say it – and I became very well-acquainted.

During one Sunday service, I was introduced to *Iva Michelle Russell*. She, too, became a dear friend as we had so much in common as fellow *"warriors"* who were trying so hard to be the voice of so many who had simply given up trying to be heard by elected officials and the VA.

Michelle asked me to offer a few comments at the 2013 *Monteagle Memorial Day Tribute* in honor of all Veterans and their families. *It was an honor to do so.*

After not seeing Randy for almost a year, I received an unexpected phone call from him one night. I, of course, was very happy to hear from him.

He asked if he could visit me in Tennessee over Memorial Day weekend. *I immediately said, "Yes!"*

Randy knocked on the door of the cottage and greeted me with a beautiful plant and a smile – one I had missed every day for the previous year.

We went on a hiking adventure that afternoon and "found" each other again. In many ways, we were never lost as we always loved each other. We had simply taken a few wrong detours. GOD has a way of bringing those misguided steps full circle.

We began making plans for me to return to Georgia in the next few months.

Following my comments at the *Monteagle Memorial Day Tribute*, Michelle asked if I would consider being the key note speaker at the June *Grundy County/Marion County Republican Women's Club* meeting. While I am not a professional speaker, I immediately accepted her offer.

I could speak about the VA's indifference in my sleep.

Iva Michelle Russell   E. Denise Caldon

I recall driving to the event in pouring rain. As I tried to dry myself off and prepare to speak, I suddenly noticed Michelle had a gentleman there with a video camera ready to film my speech! Michelle had plans, which she did, to submit my one-hour speech to *YouTube*, now available worldwide.

OUR DAILY REMINDER....

"One detour doesn't cancel your destination."
- Sarah Sarah Jakes, Author

CHAPTER VIII.
"VETERANS STILL STRUGGLE WITH A BROKEN VA"

According to Amber Smith, Washington Examiner Reporter, *"Veterans still struggle with a Broken VA."*

Excerpt from November 2014 below:

"The $16.3 billion VA reform bill was signed into law in August with high hopes. Key parts of the law had the potential to tackle the VA's most pressing issues, including accountability and private healthcare options. A broken bureaucracy was given every necessary tool to fix itself."

"But to date, little or nothing has been accomplished with the new VA powers granted by the reform law."

http://www.washingtonexaminer.com/veterans-still-struggle-with-a-broken-va/article/2555993

A FOX News release reported:

"Congress is turning up the heat on President Obama to cut the backlog of Veterans Affairs disability claims, which has gone up by 2,000 percent while the agency's budget has increased by 40 percent over the past four years. A bipartisan group of House lawmakers is the latest to call upon the president to be more aggressive, sending a letter this week asking him to "take direct action."

http://www.foxnews.com/politics/2013/06/01/democrats-and-republican-in-both-chamber-press-obama-to-end-backlog-veterans/print#ixzz2VYSmTCyK

Bryant Jordan, Military.com, reported on 5 September 2014 the following report entitled, **"Congress to Press VA on Claims Appeals Process:**

"The focus on the Board of Veterans Appeals comes as the VA works at restoring trust to a department seriously shaken by confirmed reports of secret wait lists, systemic manipulation of patient data and instances of veterans dying before getting to see a doctor.

160.

Rep. Mike Coffman, R-Colorado, told Military.com *"the VA needs to ensure a veteran's appeal claim is processed expeditiously and accurately so they receive the care they need and deserve."*

http://www.military.com/daily-news/2014/09/05/congress-to-press-va-on-claims-appeals-process.html'

It is important to remember that this critical VA Claims backlog is not a *Democratic* or a *Republican* issue – it is an **"AMERICAN"** issue.

What the media *fails* to mention is that the horrific VA Claims backlog is *not* just an issue following the last two wars this nation launched in the past decade – *it also includes the Vietnam War and others.*

Our family's long journey with the VA Claims System was featured worldwide on the website of a younger generation of Veterans Widows called *American Widow Project* in June 2012 and *The Veterans Site* in 2013.

They can be viewed at:

http://americanwidowproject.org/stories/a-vietnam-veterans-widow/

http://theveteranssite.greatergood.com/clickToGive/vet/story/the-impossible-dream-sung-at-our-wedding-in-1980-a-vietnam-veterans-widows-story772

After filing countless VA DIC Spousal Benefits Claim forms, documents, obtaining medical assessments, attending legal proceedings in Chapel Hill, NC, Atlanta, GA and Washington, D.C. and sending hundreds of emails and faxes to VA officials and legislators asking them to address the unquestionable fraudulent, illegal and horrific injustice our family has suffered - which continues today - *still unresolved.*

When I moved to Tennessee in August 2012, I had my VA file moved to Nashville. I received an email from a top official at the Georgia VA Regional Office (name withheld). He had been following my VA Claim for years and wrote to me and said:

"I wish you well and pray that you will get everything you are entitled to. If it were up to me I would write you a check today."

Even he – a top official with the VA Regional Office in Atlanta – was discouraged with the VA Claims System and his own colleagues for not admitting their horrific injustice to my family for now nineteen years.

He, too, could do nothing.

I have been told over the years by other VA representatives that the VA Claims System has a reputation of taking every step possible **to never admit they made a mistake,** and, in my case, allowed themselves to be scammed for now nineteen years by an individual who, based on law, **should be federally charged for falsifying official VA DIC Spousal Benefits documents.**

163.

My hope is that by my telling our family's story in a book - and through future speaking opportunities - I can help *"educate"* and open up much needed dialog to find critical changes and solutions so desperately needed in the VA Claims System.

I want our Family's story to be one Veterans and their families can learn from as they, too, face the realities of insurmountable paperwork that will move from one VA desk to another for years – while their family tries so desperately to find a way to put food on the table, keep the lights from being shut off, and raise their children alone – *as I did for years.*

I received a call on 23 Feb 2013 from my Bethesda, MD attorney who stated: ***"The TN VA Regional Office wants another sixty days to address the U. S. Court of Appeals for Veterans Claims ruling dated 3 September 2010 and the Board of Veterans Appeals ruling on 12 September 2012. The "sixty days" will begin the date of the letter."***

While I have lost count on how many times over the last nineteen years I have heard **"sixty more days"** from the Georgia VA Regional Office in Atlanta, the Board of Veterans Appeals in Washington, D.C., and the TN VA Regional Office in Nashville – **I will remain hopeful** – *with enough voices being heard nationwide* – **yours included**.....the serious issues at the VA Claims System will be addressed, changed and improved for thousands of brave Veterans, Widows and their families – *who have sacrificed so much for our Country's freedom.*

It is now November 2015..... *I am still waiting.*

You may recall the breach of privacy in 2009 when the BVA sent my status claim report to the address of the woman from Oregon and my receiving an apology letter from the Chairman of the BVA in February 2013.

I also received a letter from the VA Portland Veterans Service Center Manager a letter *addressed to the woman in Oregon* – dated 28 January 2013 – but mailed to my address in TN. The letter states, in part:

"We have received your application for pension benefits."

I immediately called *Bergmann and Moore*. After many calls requesting a status report from the TN VA Regional Office in Nashville, my Attorneys in Bethesda, MD discovered the woman from Oregon had now applied for my VA Pension Benefits! And, the TN VA Regional Office had sent my file to the VA Pension Center in Philadelphia with my TN address!!!

I am not making this stuff up!

The TN VA Regional Office sending my VA file to Philadelphia after two "rare" *Joint Motions for Remand* (2010 U. S. Court of Appeals for Veterans Claims; 2012 Board of Veterans Appeals) from Washington, D.C. is another example of the critical lack of communication and **"checks and balances"** within the VA Claims System that results in the continued sacrifices of so many Veterans and their families.

What I have described to you is the norm for the majority of Veterans and their Families who file VA Claims.

After learning of my VA file being sent to Philadelphia by the TN VA Regional Office - and with discouragement from my Bethesda, MD attorneys to *"not get elected officials involved as it slows the process down even further that results in nothing more than form letters"* - I reached out to officials in Washington, D.C.

In response to my letter to **The White House,** on 30 April 2013, I received a letter from *Steven L. Keller,* **Acting Chairman of the Board of Veterans Affairs in Washington, D.C.,** stating that he had forwarded my correspondence to the TN VA Regional Office in Nashville for their review and direct reply to me.

I never heard from the TN VA Regional Office.

Mr. Keller further stated; *"The law requires that all claims which are remanded by the Board for additional development must be handled in an expeditious manner under 38 U.S.C. 5109B and 7112."*

I would like to ask Mr. Keller: *"If the law requires "expeditious manner" in Claims Remanded – given that my 18-year old Claim has been remanded twice – who in the VA is enforcing this law and ensuring its compliance for Veterans and their Families?"*

My hope had been the Tennessee VA Regional Office would set an example for VA Regional Offices across the nation by correcting the unquestionable and legal injustice made by the VA Regional Office in Georgia.

It would have sent a powerful message and would have been a wonderful closing chapter in my book. *Again, the TN VA Regional Office did nothing.*

I was told by a knowledgeable source, *"VA Regional Offices will not override unquestionable errors of their fellow VA representatives"* regardless of the dire consequences and continued sacrifices to the Veteran and their family. Our family's long battle with the VA is a prime example.

I have learned through my challenges through the VA and the Georgia Board of Regents of the University System of Georgia, one must steadfastly hold on to ones beliefs and values – no matter the circumstances – *or the cost.*

OUR DAILY REMINDERS...

"It doesn't matter if a million people tell you what you can't do, or if ten million tell you no. If you get one yes from GOD, that's all you need."
                    - Tyler Perry, playwright, actor and film director

"Within our own suffering can grow the compassion and wisdom to ease the suffering of others."
                    – Small Miracles for Women

Macon woman a widow still at war

Readers of Tom Philpott's Military Update column sound off.

I want to applaud the three widows of military retirees for their lawsuit to force the Department of Defense to pay surviving spouses who remarried at 57 or older full Survivor Benefit Plan on top of their VA Dependency and Indemnity Compensation (DIC).

I have been filing document after document for over 10 years now, and finally have a hearing set for April before the Board of Veterans' Appeals in Washington, D.C. I could write a book about my family's battle with VA red tape. As my son wrote in a support letter to the VA, "this is a small battle compared to the war my Mother has already won." He was referring to years of experimental chemotherapies before my husband's death following diagnosis of Grade IV, non-Hodgkin's lymphoma which the VA had certified as "service-related due to his exposure to Agent Orange."

It has been 10 years since he died and I am still not receiving DIC spousal benefits due to the total indifference and disregard of countless VA representatives. One VA representative told me, "We have too many cases like yours. ... We do not get involved."

My mission is to "educate" members of House and Senate Veterans Affairs Committees to help prevent other veterans' widows from experiencing what my family has. Losing my husband was just the beginning of our sacrifice. For many of us, the Vietnam War is not over.
E. Denise Caldon
Macon

TOM PHILPOTT
Military Forum

tired.

This was the third time since my first husband died that the government said I owed them money because of their mistake. The first time was for $10,000. The second was for $13,000 when I was only drawing $1,100 a month to live on. Had my house not been paid off with my husband's life insurance, I would not have been able to buy food or medications.

This final time I filed a waiver to excuse the $13,000 because it was their mistake and caused financial hardship. The waiver request has been denied and they are withholding part of my DIC until the debt is paid.

Brave men who died in service to their country tried through SBP to see that their widows would be cared for if anything happened to them. I spent a large part of our 40-year marriage alone, raising five children, while my husband was overseas. We endured hardships because military pay was never equal to civilian pay.

Rep. Henry Brown, R-S.C., and several others have tried to get justice for military widows but so far their efforts have been shelved. Your articles will go a long way to getting attention toward this gross injustice.
Pat Johnson Dunn
Azle, Texas

AGE-62 DROP IN SURVIVOR

to 55 percent of covered retired pay, takes effect in a month. — Tom Philpott

SPACE-A FOR GRAY-AREA RETIREES

The Department of Defense should stop discriminatory practices directed at "gray area" retirees regarding space-available military travel benefits.

Why can't I take my family with me on space-available military aircraft until I'm 60 and begin receiving my reserve retirement pay?

I will never be able to take my sons with me to enjoy this benefit because we gray-area retirees are treated like second-class citizens for nonpaid military benefits.

Why did I spend 18 years in the reserves (after five years of active duty) working two jobs? It wasn't for the pittance in retirement I will receive at age 60. We earned and deserve to have the same nonmonetary benefits as active duty service members upon retirement. Travel for gray-area retirees would cost taxpayers virtually nothing.
Don Ehrich
Via e-mail

VA HOSPITAL TRIPS

I would like to know what is going on with the gas mileage reimbursement rate for veterans. My husband travels from Mount Airy, N.C., to Winston-Salem, N.C. He gets paid $15.55 but the VA takes $10 of that for themselves leaving him only $5.55 for his travel to and from the hospital.

Since when does the VA have the right to keep most of that money that is there for our veterans to travel to medical appointments? I have read and heard that the gas allowance

CHAPTER IX. "THE PERFECT STORM"

Given the fact our family has been thrown quite a few *"curves"* since their Father's initial terminal illness diagnosis in January 1987, I have been asked many times how it is my children and I always seem to find a way – often, with little hesitation - to look at the bright side every time life throws us another *"curve."*

My response is best expressed by one of my favorite Daily Reminders from *TruthFollower.com*, and one, among others, we live by every day:

"There is a blessing hidden in every trial in life, you simply have to be willing to open your heart to see them."

On 1 October 2015, another unexpected *"curve"* was thrown our way at a very fast pitch - *one good enough for the World Series*!

While the nation's weather forecast had been exceptionally bleak for some months, the rain in our area had over extended its' welcome for weeks. This particular Thursday afternoon was much like previous ones. With fallen branches, leaves and debris, Randy found keeping our yard difficult to keep recovered from the recent storms. Even the sunshine was inching its ways around the clouds trying to come out and play – *only to be swept up by a new round of "adventure!"*

As was my normal daily routine, I was sitting at my desk in front of my computer "fine-tuning" the last chapter of my manuscript. My goal for its completion had been on my agenda for some time.

Again, GOD simply had other plans……

My cell phone rang. It was my twin sister, *Dianne*, calling to simply catch up.

While I normally would take her call wherever I was at the time, for a reason I believe strongly is among the many blessings experienced that day, I stood up and walked toward the new sofa in the Living Room – located just a few feet away from my desk. I can count on one hand the number of times I have sat on this sofa before.

While deep in conversation, I suddenly heard, what I thought, was thunder. As I was looking straight ahead through the wall-size window, I came to the quick realization, the loud noise was not thunder – it was a very large, over seventy-year old pine tree falling toward the very room where I was sitting!

I quickly spoke very loudly in the phone to my sister and said, *"Call an ambulance!"*

I knew help would be needed – *and soon.*

Seconds later, the tree and the roof landed in our Living room – just inches to my left where I was sitting on the sofa. *I had frozen in place.* I was later told my freezing in place had saved my life.

I remember Randy calling my name from the Den - the room next to where I was. I slowly made my way to him through the rubble. He, too, was in shock.

We both walked away without a scratch!

Moments later, we saw where a large branch had also infiltrated the ceiling in our formal Dining Room as well. It, too, had been destroyed.

Thankfully, my twin sister, *Dianne*, had alerted her Husband, *Ron*, who was already enroute to our home to assist – during which he called a friend he felt could assist as well, *Richard Stembridge*. They are all among our many blessings still today.

Within minutes, the outside of our home was literally surrounded by Fire Fighters, Stembridge Roofing, Georgia Power, Gray Brothers Tree Service, concerned neighbors and family.

My oldest son's girlfriend, *Amanda,* came immediately as well and offered much support. When *Sean* arrived shortly, thereafter, I will always remember him saying to me how pleased he was to find me not panicking and crying with such an unexpected turn of events and loss of our home – literally.

His words were very dear and appreciated. The reality was, as our story discloses, *our family has experienced much worse......*

I even found myself smiling the rest of the entire evening and much of the time ever since – and for a very good reason.

You see, three of our young grandchildren and my daughter, *Logan,* were scheduled to arrive for a visit the very next day. The children would have been sitting in their *"Playroom"* at the very spot where the tree and roof fell less than twenty-four hours later.

Our insurance company, *Traveler's via GEICO,* recommended to us years earlier by our son, Sean, has, thus far, proven to be very true to their word. Randy and I have been living in a *Homewood Suites by Hilton* for almost a month as our home is inhabitable. *The staff has been remarkable and truly genuine. They have gone out of their way to make our unexpected stay pleasurable under very uncertain scenarios.*

We are scheduled to move to an apartment the second week of November 2015 while our home's extensive renovations begin. The date anticipated for our return home is four to six months minimum.

While living out of a suitcase for six months is *"challenging"* at times, the paperwork is tedious and waking up knowing your home is *"no more,"* **I am still smiling......*our family is safe.***

OUR DAILY REMINDER....

"We can only be said to be alive in those moments when our hearts are conscious of our treasures."
- Thornton, American Widow Project

CHAPTER X. "NEVER, NEVER, NEVER GIVE UP"

Our children are now 34, 33, and 30 years of age. They live with the fact their Father died for our nation's freedom.

SEAN, LOGAN AND BRYAN CALDON
Children of Jim & Denise Caldon

Our oldest son, *Sean.* 34, graduated from Georgia College and State University with a Digital Media Degree. He has received well-earned promotions, is climbing a strong career ladder at GEICO Insurance and has returned to college after office hours to obtain another degree.

Sean met his beautiful girlfriend, *Amanda,* in October 2014. They enjoyed their first Christmas together with *"Santa,"* my brother-in-law, Ron, who, has been on a very remarkable *"mission"* as Santa for over thirty years.

Sean has an exemplary way of expressing his love for our family. His unconditional love and support have been instrumental in the reasons I have fought this battle with the VA for so long as my three children represent the faces of thousands of children of Veterans' children who are just numbers to the VA.

Sean, being the oldest, recalls vividly the years we struggled emotionally, physically and financially; as well as the horrifying affects the experimental chemotherapies had invaded on his Father.

He remembers, well, his Father slipping away.

I still have memories I pray I will forget one day....

I mentioned earlier the piece of marble that was signed by each of us and mounted in the nineteen-foot Tennessee stone fireplace in our home in Chapel Hill. In early 2000, just before his brother, Bryan's birthday, Sean came to me and said, *"Mom, I would like very much to ask the owners of our home in Chapel Hill if they would be willing to let me give the inscribed marble slab to Bryan for his birthday."*

With Sean's permission, and with no hesitation, I wrote a letter to the Crawford family – who purchased our former home in Chapel Hill, NC we lost to foreclosure during Jim's terminal illness. I did not know how they would respond to our request.

A few weeks later, to my complete surprise, I received in the mail the marble slab from our **"Camelot"** home's Tennessee stone fireplace with our names engraved.

Sean was thrilled!

181.

He had the marble slab framed and presented this very sentimental gift to Bryan on his birthday – which Bryan displays proudly in his home today.

Sean's gift to his brother was further confirmation of the foundation of love our children have for each other – as they have been through, and overcome, so many very difficult times together.

Our daughter, *Logan*, graduated from Valdosta State University with a Psychology degree in 2005.

Now a single Mother, Logan is a Wellness Advocate for doTerra Oil Essentials and has returned to college. Her goal is to obtain an Occupational Therapy Degree to better ensure her children's future. She is an exemplary Mother and a woman of very strong Christian faith. *I could not be more proud.*

Our youngest son, *Bryan*, is thirty years old. He continues his Father's honorable Navy service and legacy. Bryan is a devoted Husband to his beautiful wife - my new "daughter" - *Ali*. They are the incredible parents of two of our five beautiful *"Grand-Blessings"* who know Randy and me as their *"Opa"* and *"Grand-Dee."*

Randy and I married on 19 October 2013. He, too, feels our family's story needs to be heard – *as do the stories and battles of all Veterans and their families.*

OUR DAILY REMINDER….

"The LOVE of a Family is life's greatest blessing."

It has been twenty eight years since I first heard the words embedded in my brain and heart forever.... *"Your husband has Stage IV, non-Hodgkin's lymphoma. He has two years to live."*

My late Husband would have been sixty-eight years old.

It has been nineteen years since I first notified the VA in Portland OR of the fraudulent VA DIC Spousal Benefits Application. I have filled out countless VA Claim forms, documents, obtained medical assessments, and attended legal proceedings in Chapel Hill, NC; Atlanta, GA; and Washington, D.C. I have a Timeline Summary of the hundreds of emails, faxes and correspondence I have sent to countless VA Claims Representatives and Officials at the Atlanta, Portland and Nashville VA Regional Offices, the Board of Veterans Appeals, members of the U.S. VA Committees asking them to address the fraudulent, illegal and horrific injustice our family has suffered - which continues today, *still unresolved.*

The VA hopes by moving files from one desk to another, and leave them there long enough, more Veterans and their families will go away.

My family is not going away.

Veterans and their families need more Americans to speak for them, *as far too many of our elected officials are not.*

While the journey our family has traveled has been a very long and difficult one, if I had known thirty-five years ago on 31 May 1980 my Husband was dying as a result of his exposure to Agent Orange, *I would have still walked down that aisle.*

While our lives are still not perfect, *as life never is,* the love our family shares with each other, and through our beautiful grandchildren, keeps us strong and forever grateful for how far we have traveled - *together.*

On behalf of all Veterans and their families, I will continue my efforts to assist in *"educating"* members of both state and federal VA Committees and all Americans about the years of no accountability by the VA Claims System our family is still experiencing, firsthand, for far too many years – as so many other Veterans and their families have and still do today.

It is important for our Congressional leaders and for all of America to truly comprehend the magnitude of the sacrifices made by our Country's brave Veterans and their families in wars that disabled and, for many families like ours, took the lives of their loved ones.

These sacrifices are, in many ways, *never ending.*

The VA's unwritten policy of ***"Stall, Deny and Hope they Die"*** - finally getting Congressional attention – has allowed the Wars our Veterans fought so bravely to continue.

For our Family, and for so many other Veterans and their Families, because of the VA Claims System, *the Vietnam War – and all wars – are not over......*

CBS News correspondent *Wyatt Andrews* reported on 22 February 2015 *"Whistleblowers: Veterans cheated out of benefits."*

Excerpts from the CBS Report:

"But a CBS News investigation has found widespread mismanagement of claims, resulting in veterans being denied the benefits they earned, and many even dying before they get an answer from the VA, reports CBS News correspondent Wyatt Andrews."

"Five whistleblowers at the Oakland, California, Veterans Benefits office told CBS News that Stafford's claim is one of more than 13,000 informal claims filed between 1996 and 2009 that ended up stashed in a file cabinet and ignored until 2012."

"The VA declined CBS News' repeated interview requests. It did admit to widespread problems in the handling of claims."

http://www.cbsnews.com/news/veteran-benefits-administration-mismanagement-uncovered-in-investigation/

As President Ronald Reagan reminds us....

"Freedom is never more than one generation away from extinction. We didn't pass it to our children in the bloodstream. It must be fought for, protected, and handed on for them to do the same."

Our nation's VA Claims System needs to do the same - *"Fight, Protect, and Hand Down"* to all generations of Veterans and their families their rightful benefits promised to them by our government - promises that many Veterans and their families have not been able to depend on for far too many years. Our Family is one of many.

189.

As the lyrics in Lee Greenwood's song, **"GOD Bless the USA"** say so beautifully….

"I'm proud to be an American, where at least I know I'm free. And I won't forget the men who died, who gave that right to me."

While our Congress is "divided," each American needs to ask themselves…

"Would you ask a brave soldier returning from the battlefield or laying on their deathbed dying from injuries sustained defending your freedom and the freedom of your loved ones…

"Are you a Republican or a Democrat?"

Our Congressional elected officials in Washington and in each State need to remember with each step they take walking down the corridors of the nation's Capitols, sitting behind their desk in comfortable surroundings, dining with their fellow colleagues, enjoying gifts from lobbyists, strategizing their next move to win controversial political party issues, and sleeping well at night in the comfort of their various homes knowing they have a secure income, guaranteed health insurance and pensions for life...... *Veterans and their families make indescribable sacrifices and offer their lives to enable each of them to have these privileges.*

In return, our Nation's Congress and State's General Assemblies have allowed the VA's unwritten policy to ***"Stall, Deny and Hope they Die"*** to continue....

I will always love our Country – as my late Husband was one of those men ***"who died, who gave that right to me."*** However, like an increasing number of Americans, *I cannot say I always love our government.*

Our youngest son, *Bryan*, wrote two incredible letters to the VA in 2006 and 2007. In referring to the long battle I have fought with the VA, he wrote, in part:

"I personally lost hope and never thought that it would happen. Fortunately my mother is not a quitter and she wants to make things right. I cannot even begin to describe her drive on this case, it really amazes me and I am very proud of her for it. Recently I found out that more and more people are backing up my mother on this matter and that people are starting to realize that my mother is the person that deserves the VA benefits. I do again have hope that some righteousness will come from this matter."

On Friday, 27 February 2015, I received a phone call from Ms. Angela Redmond, *Bergmann and Moore* Attorney firm – a firm who has graciously and diligently fought for many years these most recent battles with me from their office in Bethesda, MD. They are still fighting our two decade battle with the VA with us today.

They received notice that the Board of Veterans Appeals, again, *denied my Claim......*

As one VA Representative stated to me, *"Denise, if the Board of Veterans Appeals admit the unquestionable error and blatant mistake by the Atlanta and Portland VA Regional Offices for the past nineteen years in your case, it would open a flood of more claims in which they have done the same."*

In other words, the VA continues to, *"Stall, Deny and Hope I Die."*

I received another call on 11 June 2015 from Angela Redmond who stated *Bergmann and Moore* will be submitting my second Appeal to this latest Board of Veterans Appeals Denial by the 24 June 2015 deadline.

The fact the Board of Veterans Appeals will not address properly the U. S. Court of Appeals for Veterans Claims' ruling in September 2010 in which they remanded (vacated) the Board of Veteran's initial Denial in 2008 further represents the noncompliance of a broken system to which there is little recourse.

Based on legal record, *BVA Judge Harvey Roberts,* et al, do not want to open the *"Pandora's Box"* mentioned to me by the DAV representative at my Hearing in April 2008. While our family's battle with the VA is among thousands of other VA claims backlogged, with many Veterans and their families simply giving up - *I never will.*

It is the lives and challenges of our Nations' Veterans and the often unknown sacrifices of their families which allows each of us to enjoy the freedoms so many Americans take for granted.

As you come across Veterans who speak of their service or see Active Duty Troops in uniform and their family members, I ask that you remember - *Veterans Day* **and** *Memorial Day* are everyday – *not just one day a year.*

Stop. Take a moment. *"Salute"* them.

Thank them for _your_ freedom.

It is not free.

I will continue to believe one day our Congress and our Country will finally listen to the concerns and voices of thousands of Veterans and their families – like ours – *as we are real people, real families.*

Veterans and their families are not just file numbers.

When referring to the years we watched my children's Father slowly die from his exposure to Agent Orange, our struggle financially after his death in 1996, and my nineteen year battle with the VA Claims System with their unwritten policy to *"Stall, Deny and Hope They Die,"* our oldest son, *Sean*, wrote in one of his many support letters to the Board of Veterans Appeals, dated 3 September 2006........

"I hope my Mother realizes that this legal fight is a minor battle in comparison to the war that she has already won."

Our family's trust and strong faith has allowed GOD to guide our family through treacherous events, overwhelming challenges and unexpected detours.

It is now November 2015, and our family's almost two decade *"battle"* with the VA Claims System continues.

While a positive Board of Veteran's Appeals' decision - *expected any day* - would help our Family finally find closure to a very long chapter in our lives, we no longer depend on the Board of Veterans Appeals to make a decision based on the truth for our happiness.

We know the truth.

We live it.

Like most American families, our financial struggles continue. However, as a Family who has overcome so many trials together, we could never be any *"richer"* in the ways that truly matter.

My hope in sharing our family's long battle with the VA Claims System is to encourage and assist thousands of other Veterans and their families to find the strength they, too, need to continue their own battles with the VA - as our family is doing still today.

To all Veterans, their families and all people of all Nations, always remember…with passion, determination, conviction, optimism, faith and unconditional love for each other, you, too, will come to know, the *"Impossible Dream,"* is, indeed, **Possible!**

"GOD Bless the USA!"…

GOD Bless You….!

Denise

OUR DAILY REMINDER….

"Never, Never, Never Give Up."
                                                        - Winston Churchill

198.

ACKNOWLEDGEMENTS

While I have not named every one of the many family members, friends, and legal representatives who have been such an integral part and support for my children and me for over two decades in the vast number of trials we have endured during and following their Father's service-related death, please know, without each of you, I would not be sharing our family's story today.

I have saved all the expressive letters of support sent to the VA from my children, family and friends and the memorable cards from our beautiful children expressing love and gratitude. My hope is they will be shared one day to assist future generations to more fully understand the critical need for our nation, our families, our Congress, and our Veterans Administration to stand together as *"one voice"* in our support of all Veterans and their families who have sacrificed so much and, for so many, have given their lives for our nation's freedom.

Randy Sorkness
Sean Caldon and Amanda Duke
Logan, Hannah, Colin and Matthew Jones
Bryan, Ali, Conor and Charlotte Caldon
Ron and Dianne Clark
Jerry and Janie Doyal
Mary Edenfield Gibbs
James F. Smith, Jr., M.D.
The American Widow Project - Taryn Davis
Angie Allison
Bergmann & Moore, LLC:

Glenn R. Bergmann Joseph R. Moore
Bryan Andersen Alicia Guidi
Ashton Habighurst Rachelle Plotkin
Angela Redmond Liz Robbins

Andrea Timashenka
Debbie Blankenship
Todd Brandenburg
Jeff Chirico
Concerned Veterans for America - *Pete Hegseth*
Dan Cravey
Don Ewalt
Carl and Jackie Franklin
Elizabeth Hegberg
Denise Herring
Stephen F. Humphreys
Pastor Baxter Hurley
Curt Jones
Dr. J. Gregory Jones
Dan and Kim Keller
Patty Watson Kovacevich
Molly Lewis
Chance Melvin
Representative Jeff Miller
Susan Mincey
Cathy Moniot
Pastor Bob Moon

Christopher Moorman
Richard and Peggy Partin
Isiah Robinson
Versie Rouse
Iris Rudder
Iraq and Afghanistan Veterans of America (IAVA)
Iva Michelle Russell
Dr. Carolyn Schroeder
Bill Simon
Sabrina Smith
Carol Sorkness
Rick and Kristy Sorkness
Richard Stembridge
Thomas and Anna Thibeault
The Thornton Family
Sally Thomas
The Veterans Site
Veterans for Common Sense
Vietnam Veterans of America
Lisa Wagner
Jim Walls
Gay Weber
Widows of War Memorial
Ruth Wiggins
Alan Wood
Nick Caya, Word-2-Kindle.com

OUR DAILY REMINDER....

True friendship isn't about being there when it's convenient - it's about being there when it's not."   - Author Unknown

Photos below of Jim and our children during his experimental chemotherapy treatments which, ultimately, along with his PTSD, caused weight and hair loss and his mental decline.

Our children, Sean, Logan and Bryan, at Easter on our
land in Chapel Hill one year prior to our being told their
Father was dying; Sean, Logan and Bryan in
Charleston, SC where Bryan began his Navy service.

Bryan in front of our home we built for over ten years
in Chapel Hill, NC –
lost to foreclosure during his Father's
terminal illness from Agent Orange.

Photos above taken a few years after the children and I had to move to Georgia and following my Husband's death on 17 July 1996.

Sean, Logan & Bryan
High School Graduation Photos

Youngest Son, Bryan, and wife, Ali; Sean and Bryan walking up the steps *together* at the State Capitol to take family photos before Bryan and Ali's wedding - *very symbolic*

VETERAN'S WIDOW
AUTHOR

Elizabeth Denise Caldon Sorkness
C: 478.731.5576   Email: cotn712@aol.com
http://www.linkedin.com/in/denisesorkness

VA File Number: XC 28 918 810   CALDON, James A.
U. S. Court of Appeals Docket No. 08-4275

Caldon Family's VA story featured nationwide June 2012
http://americanwidowproject.org/stories/a-vietnam-veterans-widow/

http://theveteranssite.greatergood.com/clickToGive/vet/story/the-impossible-dream-sung-at-our-wedding-in-1980-a-vietnam-veterans-widows-story772

YouTube Part One:
http://www.youtube.com/watch?v=Yte6Y8PRsns&list=PLvg8pV7uZkqoqNInDBBW2-3pF5-ZT_3Lg

YouTube Part Two:
http://www.youtube.com/watch?v=4Ecs6aoCf-s&list=PLvg8pV7uZkqoqNInDBBW2-3pF5-ZT_3Lg

ISSUE:

1. Service connection for the cause of death.
2. Eligibility to Dependents' Educational Assistance under 38 U.S.C. chapter 35.

EVIDENCE:

Contents of the veteran's VA Claim File including death certificate.

DECISION:

1. Service connection for the cause of death is granted.
2. Basic eligibility to Dependents' Educational Assistance is established.

REASONS AND BASES:

1. The death of a veteran will be considered as having been due to a service-connected disability when the evidence establishes that such disability was either the primary or contributory cause of death.

The cause of death is recorded as: thalamic hemorrhage due to or as a consequence of possible aspergillus infection due to or as a consequence of immunosuppression. The death certificate also identifies lymphoma status post chemotherapy and bone marrow transplant as other significant conditions contributing to death but not resulting in the underlying cause given above. Prior to his death the veteran established service connection for non-Hodgkin's lymphoma due to herbicide exposure in Vietnam. Service connection for the cause of the veteran's death is granted since evidence shows that it was related to military service.

2. Eligibility to Dependents' Educational Assistance is derived from a veteran who was discharged under other than dishonorable conditions and has a permanent and total service-connected disability; or a permanent and total disability was in existence at the time of death; or the veteran died as a result of a service-connected disability. Basic eligibility to Dependents' Educational Assistance is granted as the evidence shows the veteran died as a result of a service-connected disability.

DEPARTMENT OF VETERANS AFFAIRS
Chairman, Board of Veterans' Appeals
Washington, DC 20420

APR 3 0 2013

In Reply Refer To: 014CLB1215
XC 28 918 810
CALDON, James A.

Mrs. Elizabeth D. Caldon
38 Assembly Avenue
Monteagle, TN 37356

Dear Mrs. Caldon:

Thank you for your correspondence of March 14, 2013, which was addressed to President Barack H. Obama, and was received at the Board of Veterans' Appeals (Board) on April 17, 2013, concerning your appeal.

On September 7, 2012, the Board remanded your case. The remand action was necessary to assist you with the development of the appeal and to ensure the record is complete. The claims file was returned to the Regional Office in Nashville, Tennessee, where development will be completed, and the appeal will be reviewed. I have forwarded your correspondence to that office for review and direct reply to you.

When the development is finished, the Regional Office will readjudicate the appeal. If any part of the decision remains unfavorable, the case will be returned to the Board for a comprehensive review of the entire record.

The law requires that all claims which are remanded by the Board for additional development must be handled in an expeditious manner under 38 U.S.C. §5109B and §7112. Should the case be transferred back to the Board, I can assure you that the appeal will be promptly adjudicated.

I hope the information I have provided is helpful. Please let me know if I can be of any further assistance.

Sincerely yours,

Steven L. Keller
Acting Chairman

cc: Joseph R. Moore, Esq.

210.

MAY 2 0 2009

In Reply Refer To: 01C2
XC 28 918 810
CALDON, James A.

The Honorable Johnny Isakson
United States Senator
One Overton Park
3625 Cumberland Boulevard, Suite 970
Atlanta, GA 30339

Dear Senator Isakson:

Thank you for your correspondence of April 24, 2009, which was sent to the Board by facsimile transmission, concerning Ms. Elizabeth D. Caldon. The purpose of your inquiry is to relay Ms. Caldon's concern with regard to the Board of Veterans' Appeals (Board) inadvertently sending information for her to the wrong address.

On December 30, 2008, the Board forwarded a letter to the Ms. Caldon regarding the status of her claim. The fact that the information was received by another appellant was done in error and constitutes a breach of Ms. Caldon's privacy. We humbly apologize for this error and a letter of apology has been written to Ms. Caldon. The address correction has been made and our records have been updated to reflect the correction.

The Board takes its responsibility to protect the private information of veterans and their dependants very seriously. We deeply regret that this situation occurred and are reviewing our policies and practices to ensure that every possible precaution is taken to keep this from happening again.

I appreciate your continued interest in Ms. Caldon's case. Please let me know if I can be of any further assistance. If Ms. Caldon would like to obtain a status update on her appeal, she may contact the Board's Status Line at 800-923-8387.

Sincerely yours,

James P. Terry

211.

• FULL NEWSPAPER ARTICLE MENTIONED IN CHAPTER V:

Published on 1/3/2003

Family takes giant leap together

By Ed Grisamore
Telegraph Columnist

Bryan Caldon is no different than any other red-blooded, American teenager.

When he turned 16 years old, he couldn't wait to get his driver's license.

Still, there was another frontier. Bryan didn't just seek wheels. He was after wings.

"I always wanted to go skydiving," he said.

Imagine his disappointment when he learned he had to be 18.

So, he has spent the past 730 days planning, preparing and saving his money. He also decided putting on a parachute was an experience he wanted to share with his family.

Today is Bryan's 18th birthday. This afternoon, he will cross the threshold of adulthood and jump out an airplane.

All in a day's work.

He will be joined by his older brother, Sean, his older sister, Logan, and friends Haley Davis and Jonathan Eden.

While her children are 14,000 feet up in the air, Denise Caldon expects her heart to be lodged somewhere in her throat.

"My whole life is jumping out of that plane," she said.

Denise will be there for "ground support" at the Skydive Atlanta facility near Thomaston.

Her mother, Betty Smith, has opted to skip the event.

"Please don't tell me the day or the time," Betty said. "Just tell me when it's over."

212.

Bryan is a senior at First Presbyterian Day School. Sean, 21, is a junior at Georgia College and State University in Milledgeville. Logan, 20, is a sophomore at Valdosta State.

Sean has been involved in much of the planning, and is just as excited as Bryan. Getting Logan on board, however, took some convincing.

"Bryan gave me this sad speech about how all he wanted for his 18th birthday was for me to go skydiving with him," she said, laughing.

Today, the two brothers will take part in an eight-hour training course to be certified for their solo jumps. The others will jump tandem with an instructor.

Denise said the skydiving is, in a way, a symbolic passage.

"It's the end of a chapter in their lives," she said. "All three will be in college next year."

When she asked why they wanted to do something so daring, they said they wanted to celebrate what they had been through to become a close-knit family.

Six years ago, her husband, Jim, died after a long battle with non-Hodgkin's lymphoma.

"They are all incredible young people who have beaten the odds through determination, perseverance and spirit," Denise said. "(They have) a passion for life, as they know first-hand how easily it can be taken away."

Denise won't be in the air herself, but she will be joined by plenty of butterflies, friends and family members.

Still, she wonders why her kids would want to do something this "crazy."

Because they are your children, her mother told her. Betty reminded Denise that she was once 18, too. She took a dare and jumped from a cliff into a swimming hole at a local kaolin pit.

"I can see the same sense of adventure in my children's eyes," said Denise. "My mom told me it's payback time."

Reach Gris at 744-4275 or egrisamore@macontel.com. Visit his Web site at http://www.grisamore.com/

213.

Whistleblowers: Veterans cheated out of benefits

Wyatt Andrews, CBS NEWS   1:06 p.m. EST February 26, 2015

The Veterans Benefits Administration provides $95 billion of entitlements each year to veterans, including disability money, pensions to vets and their surviving spouses and death benefits -- even American flags at veterans' funerals.

But a CBS News investigation has found widespread mismanagement of claims, resulting in veterans being denied the benefits they earned, and many even dying before they get an answer from the VA, reports CBS News correspondent Wyatt Andrews.

The problems at the Veteran Benefits Administration have been uncovered in the wake of last summer's scandal at a Phoenix VA hospital that rocked the Department of Veterans Affairs.

Dorrie Stafford said a letter, obtained by CBS News, **shows how badly the VA claims system is broken.**

It's dated July 29, 2014, and thanks Dorrie's husband Wayne -- an Army veteran -- for the disability claim he filed in July of 2004.

214.

The decade-long delay is just one problem; the other is that Wayne died in an accident seven years ago, without hearing a word from the VA.

"It upsets me," Dorrie said. *"Why would you suddenly, after all these years, send a letter to a dead man?"*

Five whistleblowers at the Oakland, California, Veterans Benefits office told CBS News that Stafford's claim is one of more than 13,000 informal claims filed between 1996 and 2009 that ended up stashed in a file cabinet and ignored until 2012.

Informal claims are letters from veterans expressing a desire to apply for benefits, and by law, the VA must respond with an application. *"We were getting letters from elderly veterans and from widows who were literally at the end of their life, begging for help,"* Rustyann Brown said.

She was part of a team finally assigned to process those claims two years ago and the job began, she said, with a disturbing discovery. *"Half of the veterans were dead that I screened. So almost every other piece of paper that I touched was a veteran who had already passed away,"* Brown said.

She said that means they died waiting for their first answer from the VA.

But whether the veteran was dead or still alive, brown said VA supervisors in Oakland ordered her team to mark the claims "no action necessary" and to toss them aside. Whistleblowers said that was illegal.

"The VA didn't help them. The VA didn't care about them. They took them, they put them in a file, and they stuffed them away," Brown said.

There were 13,184 veterans who were, Brown said, *"begging for help."*

When she raised her concerns, she said she was taken off the project. Then, this past summer, Brown and former VA employee Tony Silviero found a cart full of these same claims, ignored, yet again.

"We pulled 15 indiscriminately to look at; just 15," Brown said. *"Eight of them were owed money. One was owed $36,000."*

She said that was just a few months ago. Last week, the VA inspector general confirmed that because of, *"poor record keeping"* In Oakland, *"veterans did not receive....benefits to which they may have been entitled."* How many veterans is not known, because thousands of records were missing when inspectors arrived.

***Lost claims and missing records are a problem
nationwide.*** In the last year, the inspector general has
found serious issues in at least six VA benefits offices,
including unprocessed claims documents in Philadelphia,
***9,500 records sitting on employees' desks in Baltimore
and computer manipulation in Houston to make claims
look completed when they were not.***

Dorrie Stafford now lives with friends in the mountains
of Northern California, in a home with no electricity.
"They owed him an answer," she said. It's an example
of what happens when the VA conceals a file. It doesn't
just harm the veteran, it could also hurt the family.
Typically a surviving spouse is offered an American flag,
help with burial expenses or even a modest pension.
But none of that happens if there's no file.

*"I wasn't even aware there was widow benefits,
I really wasn't,"* Dorrie said.

Even if it was a modest pension of $400 a month, she
said it would help. To the whistleblowers, the lost files
also raise serious questions about whether the VA is
accurately reporting the true number of disability claims
it receives.   217.

Brown said many of the claims she discovered never even made it into the official backlog, and that was a deliberate attempt to hide them -- to make sure they never even appeared in the system.

The VA declined CBS News' repeated interview requests. It did admit to widespread problems in the handling of claims, but blamed that on the transition from a mail based system to a new electronic system. The VA said in a statement, *"electronic claims processing [has] transformed mail management for compensation claims ... greatly minimizing any risk of delays due to lost or misplaced mail."*

As for the backlog, the VA promised to fix any problem that comes to its attention. *"For any deficiencies identified, steps are taken to appropriately process the documents and correct any deficiencies."*

http://www.13wmaz.com/story/news/military/2015/02/26/ whistleblowers-veterans-cheated-out-of-benefits/24061689/

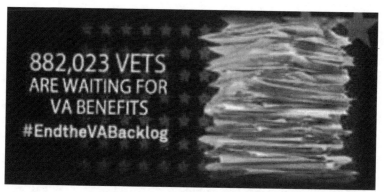

"*IAVA (Iraq and Afghanistan Veterans of America) will continue to challenge the status quo on this issue and we applaud Chairman (Jeff) Miller and the bipartisan coalition in Congress supporting the VA Accountability Act for taking action to restore trust at the VA.*"

http://thehill.com/blogs/pundits-blog/defense/249097-time-is-now-for-va-accountability-act

Our Daily Reminder….

"*A leader's job is to look into the future and see the organization not as it is, but as it should be.*"
- Jack Welch

Caldon Family's VA story featured worldwide April 2000 via website:

CALDON FAMILY - VA File No. XC 28 918 810

Denise Caldon
FROM: United States
WIDOW OF: Jim Caldon
DATE OF DEATH: 1996
PLACE OF DEATH: United States

Photo was taken one month after Jim was diagnosed with non-Hodgkin's lymphoma and given a life expectancy of two years (Jan 1987).

My husband, Jim Caldon, was a Navy Seabee who served in Vietnam in the late 60's. Shortly after we were married in 1980, Jim experienced severe stomach problems. They persisted for years. Our three children were born in 1981, 1982, and 1985. When our children were 2, 4, and 6 years of age it was determined that my husband suffered from non-Hodgkin's lymphoma - Stage IV. The prognosis was "two years." My husband lived for nine.

However the years of chemotherapy, interferon shots at home, prodigal and experimental cancer treatments resulted in my family losing him emotionally and physically before his "final" death in July of 1996 following a bone marrow transplant.

220.

After many years of testing, the VA finally classified my husband's death as *"service-related due to his exposure to Agent Orange."* My now 10-year "journey" with the VA Claims Systems for spousal benefits continues and is currently in the U. S. Court of Appeals in Washington, D.C.

Our children are now 24, 26, and 28 years of age and have lived with the fact that their Father truly died for our Country and our freedom. Our oldest son, Sean, graduated from college with a digital media degree and recently relocated back to Georgia.

Our daughter, Logan, graduated from Valdosta State University with a degree in psychology and married her college sweetheart, Brian. They live in Texas, are the proud parents of our first grandchild and are expecting their second *"blessing"* in July 2009.

Our youngest son, Bryan, is a former instructor in the Navy Nuclear Power Engineering Program in Charleston, SC where he received the *"Commanding Officer's Personal Excellence Award."* Bryan is now deployed at sea near North Korea on the USS John C. Stennis and stationed outside Bremerton Naval Base in Washington State.

I once wrote a speech for a baccalaureate class I was taking before a group of younger classmates at Macon State College. It addressed the impact of the Vietnam War on our family - and how for so many (*due to much needed changes in the VA Claims System*) *"The Vietnam War Never Ended."* I am currently being considered to speak before a U. S. Congressional Veterans Administration Committee in Washington, D. C. by Senator Isakson.

Thank you for asking us to tell our story. It means so much that someone still cares enough to ask.

Sincerely, E. Denise Caldon (Macon, GA)

Widows of War Living Memorial worldwide website *submitted on April 28, 2000 - revised 2009   *website link no longer available*

A Vietnam Veteran's Widow

June 13, 2012 by Denise, Proud Military Widow of Navy Seabee, Jim Caldon

My husband, Jim Caldon, was a Navy Seabee who served in Vietnam in the late 60's. When our children were 2, 4, and 6 years of age it was determined that my husband suffered from non-Hodgkin's lymphoma – Stage IV. The prognosis was "two years." My husband lived for nine.

However the years of chemotherapy, interferon shots at home, prodigal and experimental cancer treatments resulted in my family losing him emotionally and physically before his "final" death in July of 1996 following a bone marrow transplant.

After many years of medical testing, the VA classified my husband's death as "service-related due to his exposure to Agent Orange." Our children are now 27, 28, and 30 years of age and live with the fact that their Father died for our Country and our freedom.

Our oldest son, Sean, graduated from Georgia College and State University with a B.S. Digital Media degree. While he is now working fulltime, Sean's goal is to return to college part time to obtain his graduate degree.

Our daughter, Logan, graduated from Valdosta State University with a B.S. Psychology degree. Now a single Mother, she is raising her three young children and working on her Master's Degree.

Our youngest son, Bryan, is a former instructor in the Navy Nuclear Power Engineering Program in Charleston, SC where he received the *"2004 Commanding Officer's Personal Excellence Award."* Bryan and his beautiful bride, Ali, were married in March 2011 and are the proud parents of two.

I once wrote a speech for a baccalaureate class before a group of young people on the impact of the Vietnam War on so many families as, for so many, the Vietnam War has not ended. For our family, a reality. After nineteen years of required VA documentation, attending a VA Claims hearing before the Board of Veterans Appeals in Washington, D.C., receiving both a successful ruling by the NC Court of Appeals in Raleigh, N.C., and a Joint Motion Remand from the U. S. Court of Veterans Appeals in Washington, D.C. in September 2010, *we still wait.*

Our oldest son said to me, *"Mom, this is a small battle compared to the "war" you have already won."* My son was referring to the years we struggled watching my husband slowly die from his exposure to Agent Orange and our struggle financially after his death in 1996 – which continues due to our now 19-year battle with the Board of Veterans Appeals in Washington, D.C.

On Memorial Day, and often, I listen to the lyrics to Lee Greenwood's song, which says, *"I'm proud to be an American, where at least I know I'm free. And I won't forget the men who died, who gave that right to me"*

I know in my heart my husband is smiling down from Heaven and is very proud of his legacy as we live on in his honor and memory.

http://americanwidowproject.org/stories/a-vietnam-veterans-widow/

THE VETERANS SITE

- Featured worldwide June 2013

The Impossible Dream (Sung at our Wedding in 1980) - A Vietnam Veteran's Widow's Story

My late husband, Jim Caldon, was a Navy Seabee who served in Vietnam in the late 60's. In January 1987, when our children were 2, 4, and 6 years of age, it was discovered that my husband suffered from Stage IV non-Hodgkin's lymphoma. We were told that Jim would only live for two years. Jim died in July 1996.

The VA classified my husband's death in 1996 as "service-related due to his exposure to Agent Orange." Our children are now 28, 30 and 32 years of age and live with the fact their Father died for our freedom. I once wrote a speech for a group of young people on the impact of the Vietnam War on so many families – ours included. Because of the VA Claims System, *the Vietnam War has not ended.*

226.

On behalf of all Veterans' families that are fighting their own battle with the VA Claims System, I am speaking to the public. My latest speech is now on **YouTube** (see links below).

Our oldest son said to me, *"Mom, this is a small battle compared to the war you have already won."* Our son was referring to the years we struggled watching my husband slowly die from his exposure to Agent Orange and our struggle financially following his death – which continues today due to our now 17-year battle with the VA Claims System – even after I received a very rare "Joint Motion for Remand" from the U. S. Court of Appeals for Veterans Claims in Washington, D.C. in September 2010.

My VA file is simply moved from one VA desk to another.

One VA representative in Washington, D.C. told me in 2008 the VA's unwritten policy is, **"Stall, Deny and Hope They Die."** I am now writing a book about our family's long battle with the VA. The VA's unwritten policy is the title.

For our family, and for many others, *"Memorial Day"* and *"Veterans Day"* are every day.

I often remember the lyrics to Lee Greenwood's song which says, *"I'm proud to be an American, where at least I know I'm free. And I won't forget the men who died, who gave that right to me."* My late Husband was one. Our Country's freedom is not free.....

I know in my heart my children's Father is smiling down from Heaven and is very proud of his legacy with our incredible children who all live believing one day *"The Impossible Dream"* will be possible.

http://theveteranssite.greatergood.com/clickToGive/vet/story/the-impossible-dream-sung-at-our-wedding-in-1980-a-vietnam-veterans-widows-story772

YouTube Part One:
http://www.youtube.com/watch?v=Yte6Y8PRsns&list=PLvg8pV7uZkqoqNInDBBW2-3pF5-ZT_3Lg

YouTube Part Two:
http://www.youtube.com/watch?v=4Ecs6aoCf-s&list=PLvg8pV7uZkqoqNInDBBW2-3pF5-ZT_3Lg

Made in the USA
Charleston, SC
14 June 2016